As usual the [...]
educating cit[...]
and the fundamental tenets of freedom. From thanking
God for our liberties to the creation of Precinct Committee Officers, the constitution lays out the boundaries of
state and local government—those that affect our daily
lives—thus protecting our God-given unalienable rights
to life, liberty and property, often more effectively than
the U.S. Constitution. Everyone should read this critical
document so that we may leave future generations a better
State than the one we inherited.

Rep. Matt Shea, 4th District
House of Representatives
Washington State Legislature

If we are to be governed by the rule of law rather than
by what Judge Learned Hand called a "bevy of Platonic
guardians," we need to pay closer attention to what the
Constitution actually says. The Freedom Foundation de-
serves our gratitude for this important contribution.

David K. DeWolf
Professor of Law
Gonzaga Law School

Everywhere I go I like to quote Article I, Section I of our state constitution. It tells us where government gets its power, it tells us the importance of citizenship, and it tells us the purpose of government. Each generation must be reminded of these things.

Rep. Hans Zeiger, 25th District
House of Representatives
Washington State Legislature

The Washington State Constitution

and

the Constitution of the United States of America

With a foreword by

Chief Justice Barbara A. Madsen

Introduction by Michael J. Reitz

Freedom Foundation

2011

ISBN: 978-0-9835440-2-9

Published in the United States by:
Freedom Foundation
P.O. Box 552
Olympia, WA 98507
www.myfreedomfoundation.com

Manufactured in the United States of America

Contents

Foreword

The Washington Constitution is a marvelous legacy of our federalist system—a system that divides sovereignty between the central government and the states. It is also a reflection of the progressive and reform movements that swept the nation in the late nineteenth century, bringing a new understanding of democracy and a desire by citizens of the West to have a greater voice in the governing process. In our divided sovereignty, the federal constitution provides a floor for the protection of individual liberties, while our state constitution provides increased protections in accord with our state's history, culture, and values. The Washington Constitution reflects the benefits of a dual system, embodying important rights spelled out in the United States Constitution while embracing such influences as Jacksonian democracy, the women's suffrage movement, the Farmer's Alliance, and the Populist movement.

As a latecomer to the Union, the drafters of the Washington Constitution had the benefit of learning from the mistakes of their eastern siblings. They also had the advantage of reformist thinking that focused on making government more responsive to the people. The protections of Washington's constitution were profoundly shaped by the various protests, reforms, and radical proposals that emerged across the country in the 1880s. This unique history finds expression in several sections of our constitution. For example, article I, section 11 was worded to address a national concern with religious influence in public schools. This concern led to a requirement by Congress that our state include prohibitions against public money or property being used for religious worship, exercise, or instruction. Similarly, the language of article I, section 16 emphasizes the importance of property ownership that spurred the movement westward. It also voices a mistrust of corporations, particularly the railroad companies, that was peculiar to western states. Concern with special privileges granted by the citizen legislature, especially to the railroads, is also reflected in the language of article I, section 12, which forbids the legislature from passing any law granting special privileges or immunities. Unlike the federal constitution, Washington's constitution sets out a right to free and equal elections and the free exercise of the right of suffrage. Other provisions guaranteeing the right to initiative, referendum and recall of public officials also bear witness to the reformist roots of our founding document.

Suffragist Abigail Scott Duniway explained that "[a]ll great uprisings of the race, looking to the establishment of a larger liberty for all the people, have first been generated in new countries, where plastic conditions adapt themselves to larger growths." Indeed, Washington was the fifth state to guarantee a woman's right to vote— ten years ahead of the Twenty-first Amendment of the United States Constitution.

Digging through treaties, studying the Organic Act, and reading editorials from the *Seattle Daily Times* and *The Morning Journal* are among the tools necessary to understanding and interpreting this unique document. The history of the country and of this region are key to providing context for the provisions of the Washington Constitution and to appreciating the conditions that motivated the decisions of its drafters, what issues needed to be addressed in the document, what rights needed to receive enhanced protection, and how the interests that led the people of the territory to seek statehood could best be protected.

In my role as a justice of the Washington State Supreme Court, I am privileged to witness our state's history of protecting individual liberties play out year after year in legal challenges brought under our state constitution. Far from a musty tome, our state constitution is alive in protecting the rights of Washington State citizens every day. It is our state constitution, not the federal constitution, that prohibits random vehicle searches at sobriety checkpoints and requires police officers to inform residents that they do not have to necessarily consent to a search of their homes. The fact that state financial aid may not be used to assist a student enrolled in any program that includes religious worship, exercise, or instruction arises only from the provisions of the state constitution. From requiring a "public use" as a prerequisite to the use of the power of eminent domain to calling out a right to privacy, the Washington Constitution offers greater protection of individual rights than what its federal counterpart provides.

This booklet is a wonderful resource for learning about our state's system of government. It is also an important reminder that our state constitution guarantees an additional layer of protection against government intrusion into the private affairs of Washington citizens.

Barbara A. Madsen
Chief Justice
Washington State Supreme Court

Introduction to the
Washington Constitution

On July 4, 1889, seventy-five constitutional delegates gathered in Olympia, Washington, to compose a state constitution. The delegates came from all walks of life; among them were lawyers, judges, doctors, teachers, politicians, and businessmen. The Washington Constitution was drafted over forty days of deliberation. The people ratified the constitution on October 1, 1889, and on November 11, 1889, President Benjamin Harrison issued a proclamation admitting Washington into the United States of America.

The first principle articulated in the Washington Constitution is its source of authority. Individual citizens are endowed with inherent freedoms that can neither be conferred nor exterminated by the state. As the opening section of the Washington Constitution declares: "All political power is inherent in the people, and governments derive their just powers from the consent of the governed, and are established to protect and maintain individual rights" (art. I, § 1). The constitution, then, is a delegation of authority from the state's sovereigns—the citizens—to the separate branches of government. The constitution serves to limit the branches of government, rather than conferring unlimited power on elected officials.

But why read the Washington Constitution? Our system of free government is founded on the consent of the governed, and it requires frequent, vigilant attention to secure our continued prosperity. As Justice Robert F. Utter wrote in 1991, state constitutions were originally intended to be the first line of defense for the protection of individual liberty, with the federal constitution acting as a secondary protection. In 1986, in the landmark case of State v. Gunwall, the Supreme Court of Washington ruled that the Washington Constitution may often extend broader protection of rights to its citizens than the U.S. Constitution. This ruling has led to numerous decisions by the court that recognize the Washington Constitution's expansive protection of individual liberty.

The Freedom Foundation is publishing Washington Constitution in order to equip the people of this state with an essential resource. Many today have discovered an interest in the original texts composed by the founders of our country and our state. These original sources inform our understanding of the role and priorities of government. When citizens are educated in the sources of their freedoms, and familiar with attempts in history to limit these freedoms, they are better equipped to recognize new encroachments.

The Washington Constitution admonishes us that a "frequent recurrence to fundamental principles is essential to the security of individual right and the perpetuity of free government" (art. I, § 32). It is our hope that this resource will expand the appreciation for the liberties we all enjoy.

Michael J. Reitz
General Counsel
Freedom Foundation

The Unique Role of
State Constitutions

State courts give life to the meaning of words in their state constitutions. They have a similar function in interpreting federal constitutions, where the federal courts have not spoken on the issues involved. Application of fundamental concepts such as personal rights, freedom of speech, private affairs, religious freedom, due process, and equal protection are often first explored in state courts and disposed of on state grounds. Decisions based on state constitutional grounds which do not grant fewer rights than the federal constitution are binding and final.

State constitutions existed in most early states prior to the adoption of the federal constitution and were originally intended as the primary devices to protect individual rights. In this role, the United States Supreme Court has looked to state decisions and has adopted such concepts as the exclusionary rule, the right to counsel, and freedom of the press.

Four decades ago there were no courses on state constitutional law taught in this state. Now all law schools in the state offer such courses. It is entirely appropriate that the people of this state be aware of the provisions of their constitution and the way in which it affects their lives.

Justice Robert F. Utter
Washington State Supreme Court
(Ret.)

The Washington State Constitution

Preamble

We, the people of the State of Washington, grateful to the Supreme Ruler of the Universe for our liberties, do ordain this constitution.

Article I
Declaration of Rights

Section 1. Political power. All political power is inherent in the people, and governments derive their just powers from the consent of the governed, and are established to protect and maintain individual rights.

Section 2. Supreme law of the land. The Constitution of the United States is the supreme law of the land.

Section 3. Personal rights. No person shall be deprived of life, liberty, or property, without due process of law.

Section 4. Right of petition and assemblage. The right of petition and of the people peaceably to assemble for the common good shall never be abridged.

Section 5. Freedom of speech. Every person may freely speak, write and publish on all subjects, being responsible for the abuse of that right.

Section 6. Oaths – Mode of administering. The mode of administering an oath, or affirmation, shall be such as may be most consistent with and binding upon the conscience of the person to whom such oath, or affirmation, may be administered.

Section 7. Invasion of private affairs or home prohibited. No person shall be disturbed in his private affairs, or his home invaded, without authority of law.

Section 8. Irrevocable privilege, franchise or immunity prohibited. No law granting irrevocably any privilege, franchise or immunity, shall be passed by the legislature.

Section 9. Rights of accused persons. No person shall be compelled in any criminal case to give evidence against himself, or be twice put in jeopardy for the same offense.

Section 10. Administration of justice. Justice in all cases shall be administered openly, and without unnecessary delay.

Section 11. Religious freedom. Absolute freedom of conscience in all matters of religious sentiment, belief and worship, shall be guaranteed to every individual, and no one shall be molested or disturbed in person or property on account of religion; but the liberty of conscience hereby secured shall not be so construed as to excuse acts of licentiousness or justify practices inconsistent with the peace and safety of the state. No public money or property shall be appropriated for or applied to any religious worship, exercise or instruction, or the support of any religious establishment: PROVIDED, HOWEVER, That this article shall not be so construed as to forbid the employment by the state of a chaplain for such of the state custodial, correctional, and mental institutions, or by a county's or public hospital district's hospital, health care facility, or hospice, as in the discretion of the legislature may seem justified. No religious qualification shall be required for any public office or employment, nor shall any person be incompetent as a witness or juror, in consequence of his opinion on matters of religion, nor be questioned in any court of justice touching his religious belief to affect the weight of his testimony. [Amendment 88, 1993 House Joint Resolution No. 4200, p 3062. Approved November 2, 1993.]

Section 12. Special privileges and immunities prohibited. No law shall be passed granting to any citizen, class of citizens, or corporation other than municipal, privileges or immunities which upon the same terms shall not equally belong to all citizens, or corporations.

Section 13. Habeas corpus. The privilege of the writ of habeas corpus shall not be suspended, unless in case of rebellion or invasion the public safety requires it.

Section 14. Excessive bail, fines and punishments. Excessive bail shall not be required, excessive fines imposed, nor cruel punishment inflicted.

Section 15. Convictions, effect of. No conviction shall work corruption of blood, nor forfeiture of estate.

Section 16. Eminent domain. Private property shall not be taken for private use, except for private ways of necessity, and for drains, flumes, or ditches on or across the lands of others for agricultural, domestic, or sanitary purposes. No private property shall be taken or damaged for public or private use without just compensation having been first made, or paid into court for the owner, and no right-of-way shall be appropriated to the use of any corporation other than municipal until full compensation therefor be first made in money, or ascertained and paid into court for the owner, irrespective of any benefit from any improvement proposed by such corporation, which compensation shall be ascertained by a jury, unless a jury be waived, as in other civil cases in courts of record, in the manner prescribed by law. Whenever an attempt is made to take private property for a use alleged to be public, the question whether the contemplated use be really public shall be a judicial question, and determined as such, without regard to any legislative assertion that the use is public: *Provided,* That the taking of private property by the state for land reclamation and settlement purposes is hereby declared to be for public use. [Amendment 9, 1919 p 385 Section 1. Approved November, 1920.]

Section 17. Imprisonment for debt. There shall be no imprisonment for debt, except in cases of absconding debtors.

Section 18. Military power, limitation of. The military shall be in strict subordination to the civil power.

Section 19. Freedom of elections. All Elections shall be free and equal, and no power, civil or military, shall at any time interfere to prevent the free exercise of the right of suffrage.

Section 20. Bail, when authorized. All persons charged with crime shall be bailable by sufficient sureties, except for capital offenses when the proof is evident, or the presumption great. Bail may be denied for offenses punishable by the possibility of life in prison upon a showing by clear and convincing evidence of a propensity for violence that creates a substantial likelihood of danger to the community or any persons, subject to such limitations as shall be determined by the legislature. [Amendment 104, 2010 Engrossed Substitute House Joint Resolution No. 4220, p 3129. Approved November 2, 2010.]

Section 21. Trial by jury. The right of trial by jury shall remain inviolate, but the legislature may provide for a jury of any number less than twelve in courts not of record, and for a verdict by nine or more jurors in civil cases in any court of record, and for waiving of the jury in civil cases where the consent of the parties interested is given thereto.

Section 22. Rights of the accused. In criminal prosecutions the accused shall have the right to appear and defend in person, or by counsel, to demand the nature and cause of the accusation against him, to have a copy thereof, to testify in his own behalf, to meet the witnesses against him face to face, to have compulsory process to compel the attendance of witnesses in his own behalf, to have a speedy public trial by an impartial jury of the county in which the offense is charged to have been committed and the right to appeal in all cases: *Provided,* The route traversed by any railway coach, train or public conveyance, and the water traversed by any boat shall be criminal districts; and the jurisdiction of all public offenses committed on any such railway car, coach, train, boat or other public conveyance, or at any station or depot upon such route, shall be in any county through which the said car, coach, train, boat or other public conveyance may pass during the trip or voyage, or in which the trip or voyage may begin or terminate. In no instance shall any accused person before final judgment be compelled to advance money or fees to secure the rights herein guaranteed. [Amendment 10, 1921 p 79 Section 1. Approved November, 1922.]

Section 23. Bill of attainder, ex post facto law, etc. No bill of attainder, ex post facto law, or law impairing the obligations of contracts shall ever be passed.

Section 24. Right to bear arms. The right of the individual citizen to bear arms in defense of himself, or the state, shall not be impaired, but nothing in this section shall be construed as authorizing individuals or corporations to organize, maintain or employ an armed body of men.

Section 25. Prosecution by information. Offenses heretofore required to be prosecuted by indictment may be prosecuted by information, or by indictment, as shall be prescribed by law.

Section 26. Grand jury. No grand jury shall be drawn or summoned in any county, except the superior judge thereof shall so order.

Section 27. Treason, defined, etc. Treason against the state shall consist only in levying war against the state, or adhering to its enemies, or in giving them aid and comfort. No person shall be convicted of treason unless on the testimony of two witnesses to the same overt act, or confession in open court.

Section 28. Hereditary privileges abolished. No hereditary emoluments, privileges, or powers, shall be granted or conferred in this state.

Section 29. Constitution mandatory. The provisions of this Constitution are mandatory, unless by express words they are declared to be otherwise.

Section 30. Rights reserved. The enumeration in this Constitution of certain rights shall not be construed to deny others retained by the people.

Section 31. Standing army. No standing army shall be kept up by this state in time of peace, and no soldier shall in time of peace be quartered in any house without the consent of its owner, nor in time of war except in the manner prescribed by law.

Section 32. Fundamental principles. A frequent recurrence to fundamental principles is essential to the security of individual right and the perpetuity of free government.

Section 33. Recall of elective officers. Every elective public officer of the state of Washington expect [except] judges of courts of record is subject to recall and discharge by the legal voters of the state, or of the political subdivision of the state, from which he was elected whenever a petition demanding his recall, reciting that such officer has committed some act or acts of malfeasance or misfeasance while in office, or who has violated his oath of office, stating the matters complained of, signed by the percentages of the qualified electors thereof, hereinafter provided, the percentage required to be computed from the total number of votes cast for all candidates for his said office to which he was elected at the preceding election, is filed with the officer with whom a petition for nomination, or certificate for nomination, to such office must be filed under the laws of this state, and the same officer shall call a special election as provided by the general election laws of this state, and the result determined as therein provided. [Amendment 8, 1911 p 504 Section 1. Approved November, 1912.]

Section 34. Same. The legislature shall pass the necessary laws to carry out the provisions of section thirty-three (33) of this article, and to facilitate its operation and effect without delay: *Provided,* That the authority hereby conferred upon the legislature shall not be construed to grant to the legislature any exclusive power of lawmaking nor in any way limit the initiative and referendum powers reserved by the people. The percentages required shall be, state officers, other than judges, senators and representatives, city officers of cities of the first class, school district boards in cities of the first class; county officers of counties of the first, second and third classes, twenty-five per cent. Officers of all other political subdivisions, cities, towns, townships, precincts and school districts not herein mentioned, and state senators and representatives, thirty-five per cent. [Amendment 8, 1911 p 504 Section 1. Approved November, 1912.]

Section 35. Victims of crimes – Rights. Effective law enforcement depends on cooperation from victims of crime. To ensure victims a meaningful role in the criminal justice system and to accord them due dignity and respect, victims of crime are hereby granted the following basic and fundamental rights.

Upon notifying the prosecuting attorney, a victim of a crime charged as a felony shall have the right to be informed of and, subject to the discretion of the individual presiding over the trial or court proceedings, attend trial and all other court proceedings the defendant has the right to attend, and to make a statement at sentencing and at any proceeding where the defendant's release is considered, subject to the same rules of procedure which govern the defendant's rights. In the event the victim is deceased, incompetent, a minor, or otherwise unavailable, the prosecuting attorney may identify a representative to appear to exercise the victim's rights. This provision shall not constitute a basis for error in favor of a defendant in a criminal proceeding nor a basis for providing a victim or the victim's representative with court appointed counsel. [Amendment 84, 1989 Senate Joint Resolution No. 8200, p 2999. Approved November 7, 1989.]

Article II
Legislative Department

Section 1. Legislative powers, where vested. The legislative authority of the state of Washington shall be vested in the legislature, consisting of a senate and house of representatives, which shall be called the legislature of the state of Washington, but the people reserve to themselves the power to propose bills, laws, and to enact or reject the same at the polls, independent of the legislature, and also reserve power, at their own option, to approve or reject at the polls any act, item, section, or part of any bill, act, or law passed by the legislature.

(a) Initiative: The first power reserved by the people is the initiative. Every such petition shall include the full text of the measure so proposed. In the case of initiatives to the legislature and initiatives to the people, the number of valid signatures of legal voters required shall be equal to eight percent of the votes cast for the office of governor at the last gubernatorial election preceding the initial filing of the text of the initiative measure with the secretary of state.

Initiative petitions shall be filed with the secretary of state not less than four months before the election at which they are to be voted upon, or not less than ten days before any regular session of the legislature. If filed at least four months before the election at which they are to be voted upon, he shall submit the same to the vote of the people at the said election. If such petitions are filed not less than ten days before any regular session of the legislature, he shall certify the results within forty days of the filing. If certification is not complete by the date that the legislature convenes, he shall provisionally certify the measure pending final certification of the measure. Such initiative measures, whether certified or provisionally certified, shall take precedence over all other measures in the legislature except appropriation bills and shall be either enacted or rejected without change or amendment by the legislature before the end of such regular session. If any such initiative measures shall be enacted by the legislature it shall be subject to the referendum petition, or it may be enacted and referred by the legislature to the people for approval or rejection at the next regular election. If it is rejected or if no action is taken upon it by the legislature before the end of such regular session, the secretary of state shall submit it to the people for approval or rejection at the next ensuing regular general election. The legislature may reject any measure so proposed by initiative petition and propose a different one dealing with the same subject, and in such event both measures shall be submitted by the secretary of state to the people for approval or rejection at the next ensuing regular general election. When conflicting measures are submitted to the people the ballots shall be so printed that a voter can express separately by making one cross (X) for each, two preferences, first, as between either measure and neither, and secondly, as between one and the other. If the majority of those voting on the first issue is for neither, both fail, but in that case the votes on the second issue shall nevertheless be carefully counted and made public. If a majority voting on the first issue is for either, then the measure receiving a majority of the votes on the second issue shall be law.

(b) Referendum. The second power reserved by the people is the referendum, and it may be ordered on any act, bill, law, or any part thereof passed by the legislature, except such laws as may be necessary for the immediate preservation of the public peace, health or safety, support of the state government and its existing public institutions, either by petition signed by the required percentage of the legal voters, or by the legislature as other bills are enacted: *Provided,* That the legislature may not order a referendum on any initiative measure enacted by the legislature under the foregoing subsection (a). The number of valid signatures of registered voters required on a petition for referendum of an act of the legislature or any part thereof, shall be equal to or exceeding four percent of the votes cast for the office of governor at the last gubernatorial election preceding the filing of the text of the referendum measure with the secretary of state.

(c) No act, law, or bill subject to referendum shall take effect until ninety days after the adjournment of the session at which it was enacted. No act, law, or bill approved by a majority of the electors voting thereon shall be amended or repealed by the legislature within a period of two years following such enactment: *Provided,* That any such act, law, or bill may be amended within two years after such enactment at any regular or special session of the legislature by a vote of two-thirds of all the members elected to each house with full compliance with section 12, Article III, of the Washington Constitution, and no amendatory law adopted in accordance with this provision shall be subject to referendum. But such enactment may be amended or repealed at any general regular or special election by direct vote of the people thereon.

(d) The filing of a referendum petition against one or more items, sections, or parts of any act, law, or bill shall not delay the remainder of the measure from becoming operative. Referendum petitions against measures passed by the legislature shall be filed with the secretary of state not later than ninety days after the final adjournment of the session of the legislature which passed the measure on which the referendum is demanded. The veto power of the governor shall not extend to measures initiated by or referred to the people. All elections on measures referred to the people of the state shall be had at the next succeeding regular general election following the filing of the measure with the secretary of state, except when the legislature shall order a special election. Any measure initiated by the people or referred to the people as herein provided shall take effect and become the law if it is approved by a majority of the votes cast thereon: *Provided,* That the vote cast upon such question or measure shall equal one-third of the total votes cast at such election and not otherwise. Such measure shall be in operation on and after the thirtieth day after the election at which it is approved. The style of all bills proposed by initiative petition shall be: "Be it enacted by the people of the State of Washington." This section shall not be construed to deprive any member of the legislature of the right to introduce any measure. All such petitions shall be filed with the secretary of state, who shall be guided by the general laws in submitting the same to the people until additional legislation shall especially provide therefor. This section is self-executing, but legislation may be enacted especially to facilitate its operation.

(e) The legislature shall provide methods of publicity of all laws or parts of laws, and amendments to the Constitution referred to the people with arguments for and against the laws and amendments so referred. The secretary of state shall send one copy of the publication to each individual place of residence in the state and shall make such additional distribution as he shall determine necessary to reasonably assure that each voter will have an opportunity to study the measures prior to election. [Amendment 72, 1981 Substitute Senate Joint Resolution No. 133, p 1796. Approved November 3, 1981.]

Section 1(a). Initiative and referendum, signatures required. [Stricken by Amendment 72, 1981 Substitute Senate Joint Resolution No. 133, p 1796. Approved November 3, 1981.]

Section 2. House of representatives and senate. The house of representatives shall be composed of not less than sixty-three nor more than ninety-nine members. The number of senators shall not be more than one-half nor less than one-third of the number of members of the house of representatives. The first legislature shall be composed of seventy members of the house of representatives, and thirty-five senators.

Section 3. The census. [Repealed by Amendment 74, 1983 Substitute Senate Joint Resolution No. 103, p 2202. Approved November 8, 1983.]

Section 4. Election of representatives and term of office. Members of the house of representatives shall be elected in the year eighteen hundred and eighty-nine at the time and in the manner provided by this Constitution, and shall hold their offices for the term of one year and until their successors shall be elected.

Section 5. Elections, when to be held. The next election of the members of the house of representatives after the adoption of this Constitution shall be on the first Tuesday after the first Monday of November, eighteen hundred and ninety, and thereafter, members of the house of representatives shall be elected biennially and their term of office shall be two years; and each election shall be on the first Tuesday after the first Monday in November, unless otherwise changed by law.

Section 6. Election and term of office of senators. After the first election the senators shall be elected by single districts of convenient and contiguous territory, at the same time and in the same manner as members of the house of representatives are required to be elected; and no representative district shall be divided in the formation of a senatorial district. They shall be elected for the term of four years, one-half of their number retiring every two years. The senatorial districts shall be numbered consecutively, and the senators chosen at the first election had by virtue of this Constitution, in odd numbered districts, shall go out of office at the end of the first year; and the senators, elected in the even numbered districts, shall go out of office at the end of the third year.

Section 7. Qualifications of legislators. No person shall be eligible to the legislature who shall not be a citizen of the United States and a qualified voter in the district for which he is chosen.

Section 8. Judges of their own election and qualification – Quorum. Each house shall be the judge of the election, returns and qualifications of its own members, and a majority of each house shall constitute a quorum to do business; but a smaller number may adjourn from day to day and may compel the attendance of absent members, in such manner and under such penalties as each house may provide.

Section 9. Rules of procedure. Each house may determine the rules of its own proceedings, punish for contempt and disorderly behavior, and, with the concurrence of two-thirds of all the members elected, expel a member, but no member shall be expelled a second time for the same offense.

Section 10. Election of officers. Each house shall elect its own officers; and when the lieutenant governor shall not attend as president, or shall act as governor, the senate shall choose a temporary president. When presiding, the lieutenant governor shall have the deciding vote in case of an equal division of the senate.

Section 11. Journal, publicity of meetings – Adjournments. Each house shall keep a journal of its proceedings and publish the same, except such parts as require secrecy. The doors of each house shall be kept open, except when the public welfare shall require secrecy. Neither house shall adjourn for more than three days, nor to any place other than that in which they may be sitting, without the consent of the other.

Section 12. Sessions, when – Duration. (1) Regular Sessions. A regular session of the legislature shall be convened each year. Regular sessions shall convene on such day and at such time as the legislature shall determine by statute. During each odd-numbered year, the regular session shall not be more than one hundred five consecutive days. During each even-numbered year, the regular session shall not be more than sixty consecutive days.

(2) Special Legislative Sessions. Special legislative sessions may be convened for a period of not more than thirty consecutive days by proclamation of the governor pursuant to Article III, section 7 of this Constitution. Special legislative sessions may also be convened for a period of not more than thirty consecutive days by resolution of the legislature upon the affirmative vote in each house of two-thirds of the members elected or appointed thereto, which vote may be taken and resolution executed either while the legislature is in session or during any interim between sessions in accordance with

such procedures as the legislature may provide by law or resolution. The resolution convening the legislature shall specify a purpose or purposes for the convening of a special session, and any special session convened by the resolution shall consider only measures germane to the purpose or purposes expressed in the resolution, unless by resolution adopted during the session upon the affirmative vote in each house of two-thirds of the members elected or appointed thereto, an additional purpose or purposes are expressed. The specification of purpose by the governor pursuant to Article III, section 7 of this Constitution shall be considered by the legislature but shall not be mandatory.

(3) Committees of the Legislature. Standing and special committees of the legislature shall meet and conduct official business pursuant to such rules as the legislature may adopt. [Amendment 68, 1979 Substitute Senate Joint Resolution No. 110, p 2286. Approved November 6, 1979.]

Section 13. Limitation on members holding office in the state. No member of the legislature, during the term for which he is elected, shall be appointed or elected to any civil office in the state, which shall have been created during the term for which he was elected. Any member of the legislature who is appointed or elected to any civil office in the state, the emoluments of which have been increased during his legislative term of office, shall be compensated for the initial term of the civil office at the level designated prior to the increase in emoluments.

[Amendment 69, 1979 Senate Joint Resolution No. 112, p 2287. Approved November 6, 1979.]

Section 14. Same, federal or other office. No person, being a member of congress, or holding any civil or military office under the United States or any other power, shall be eligible to be a member of the legislature; and if any person after his election as a member of the legislature, shall be elected to congress or be appointed to any other office, civil or military, under the government of the United States, or any other power, his acceptance thereof shall vacate his seat, provided, that officers in the militia of the state who receive no annual salary, local officers and postmasters, whose compensation does not exceed three hundred dollars per annum, shall not be ineligible.

Section 15. Vacancies in legislature and in partisan county elective office. Such vacancies as may occur in either house of the legislature or in any partisan county elective office shall be filled by appointment by the county legislative authority of the county in which the vacancy occurs: *Provided,* That the person appointed to fill the vacancy must be from the same legislative district, county, or county commissioner or council district and the same political party as the legislator or partisan county elective officer whose office has been vacated, and shall be one of three persons who shall be nominated by the county central committee of that party, and in case a majority of the members of the county legislative authority do not agree upon the appointment within sixty days after the vacancy occurs, the governor shall within thirty days thereafter, and from the list of nominees provided for herein, appoint a person who shall be from the same legislative district, county, or county commissioner or council district and of the same political party as the legislator or partisan county elective officer whose office has been vacated, and the person so appointed shall hold office until his or her successor is elected at the next general election, and has qualified: *Provided,* That in case of a vacancy occurring after the general election in a year that the office appears on the ballot and before the start of the next term, the term of the successor who is of the same party as the incumbent may commence once he or she has qualified and shall continue through the term for which he or she was elected: *Provided,* That in case of a vacancy occurring in the office of joint senator, or joint representative, the vacancy shall be filled from a list of three nominees selected by the state central committee, by appointment by the joint action of the boards of county legislative authorities of the counties composing the joint senatorial or joint representative district, the person appointed to fill the vacancy must be from the same legislative district and of the same political party as the legislator whose office has been vacated, and in case a majority of the members of the county legislative authority do not agree upon the appointment within sixty days after the vacancy occurs, the governor shall within thirty days thereafter, and from the list of nominees provided for herein, appoint a person who shall be from the same legislative district and of the same political party as the legislator whose office has been vacated. [Amendment 96, 2003 House Joint Resolution No. 4206, p 2819. Approved November 4, 2003.]

Section 16. Privileges from arrest. Members of the legislature shall be privileged from arrest in all cases except treason, felony and breach of the peace; they shall not be subject to any civil process during the session of the legislature, nor for fifteen days next before the commencement of each session.

Section 17. Freedom of debate. No member of the legislature shall be liable in any civil action or criminal prosecution whatever, for words spoken in debate.

Section 18. Style of laws. The style of the laws of the state shall be: "Be it enacted by the Legislature of the State of Washington." And no laws shall be enacted except by bill.

Section 19. Bill to contain one subject. No bill shall embrace more than one subject, and that shall be expressed in the title.

Section 20. Origin and amendment of bills. Any bill may originate in either house of the legislature, and a bill passed by one house may be amended in the other.

Section 21. Yeas and nays. The yeas and nays of the members of either house shall be entered on the journal, on the demand of one-sixth of the members present.

Section 22. Passage of bills. No bill shall become a law unless on its final passage the vote be taken by yeas and nays, the names of the members voting for and against the same be entered on the journal of each house, and a majority of the members elected to each house be recorded thereon as voting in its favor.

Section 23. Compensation of members. Each member of the legislature shall receive for his services five dollars for each day's attendance during the session, and ten cents for every mile he shall travel in going to and returning from the place of meeting of the legislature, on the most usual route.

Section 24. Lotteries and divorce. The legislature shall never grant any divorce. Lotteries shall be prohibited except as specifically authorized upon the affirmative vote of sixty percent of the members of each house of the legislature or, notwithstanding any other provision of this Constitution, by referendum or initiative approved by a sixty percent affirmative vote of the electors voting thereon. [Amendment 56, 1971 Senate Joint Resolution No. 5, p 1828. Approved November 7, 1972.]

Section 25. Extra compensation prohibited. The legislature shall never grant any extra compensation to any public officer, agent, employee, servant, or contractor, after the services shall have been rendered, or the contract entered into, nor shall the compensation of any public officer be increased or diminished during his term of office. Nothing in this section shall be deemed to prevent increases in pensions after such pensions shall have been granted. [Amendment 35, 1957 Senate Joint Resolution No. 18, p 1301. Approved November 4, 1958.]

Section 26. Suits against the state. The legislature shall direct by law, in what manner, and in what courts, suits may be brought against the state.

Section 27. Elections – Viva voce vote. In all elections by the legislature the members shall vote viva voce, and their votes shall be entered on the journal.

Section 28. Special legislation. The legislature is prohibited from enacting any private or special laws in the following cases:

1. For changing the names of persons, or constituting one person the heir at law of another.

2. For laying out, opening or altering highways, except in cases of state roads extending into more than one county, and military roads to aid in the construction of which lands shall have been or may be granted by congress.

3. For authorizing persons to keep ferries wholly within this state.

4. For authorizing the sale or mortgage of real or personal property of minors, or others under disability.

5. For assessment or collection of taxes, or for extending the time for collection thereof.

6. For granting corporate powers or privileges.

7. For authorizing the apportionment of any part of the school fund.

8. For incorporating any town or village or to amend the charter thereof.

9. From giving effect to invalid deeds, wills or other instruments.

10. Releasing or extinguishing in whole or in part, the indebtedness, liability or other obligation, of any person, or corporation to this state, or to any municipal corporation therein.

11. Declaring any person of age or authorizing any minor to sell, lease, or encumber his or her property.

12. Legalizing, except as against the state, the unauthorized or invalid act of any officer.

13. Regulating the rates of interest on money.

14. Remitting fines, penalties or forfeitures.

15. Providing for the management of common schools.

16. Authorizing the adoption of children.

17. For limitation of civil or criminal actions.

18. Changing county lines, locating or changing county seats, provided, this shall not be construed to apply to the creation of new counties.

Section 29. Convict labor. The labor of inmates of this state shall not be let out by contract to any person, copartnership, company, or corporation, except as provided by statute, and the legislature shall by law provide for the working of inmates for the benefit of the state, including the working of inmates in state-run inmate labor programs. Inmate labor programs provided by statute that are operated and managed, in total or in part, by any profit or nonprofit entities shall be operated so that the programs do not unfairly compete with Washington businesses as determined by law. [Amendment 100, 2007 Senate Joint Resolution No. 8212, p 3143. Approved November 6, 2007.]

Section 30. Bribery or corrupt solicitation. The offense of corrupt solicitation of members of the legislature, or of public officers of the state or any municipal division

thereof, and any occupation or practice of solicitation
of such members or officers to influence their official
action, shall be defined by law, and shall be punished by
fine and imprisonment. Any person may be compelled to
testify in any lawful investigation or judicial proceeding
against any person who may be charged with having
committed the offense of bribery or corrupt solicitation,
or practice of solicitation, and shall not be permitted
to withhold his testimony on the ground that it may
criminate himself or subject him to public infamy, but
such testimony shall not afterwards be used against him
in any judicial proceeding—except for perjury in giving
such testimony—and any person convicted of either of
the offenses aforesaid, shall as part of the punishment
therefor, be disqualified from ever holding any position
of honor, trust or profit in this state. A member who has
a private interest in any bill or measure proposed or
pending before the legislature, shall disclose the fact to
the house of which he is a member, and shall not vote
thereon.

Section 31. Laws, when to take effect. [This section
stricken by Amendment 7, 1911 House Bill No. 153, p 136.
Approved November, 1912.]

Section 32. Laws, how signed. No bill shall become a
law until the same shall have been signed by the presiding
officer of each of the two houses in open session, and
under such rules as the legislature shall prescribe.

Section 33. Alien ownership. [Repealed by Amendment 42, 1965 ex.s. Senate Joint Resolution No. 20, p 2816. Approved November 8, 1966.]

Section 34. Bureau of statistics, agriculture and immigration. There shall be established in the office of the secretary of state, a bureau of statistics, agriculture and immigration, under such regulations as the legislature may provide.

Section 35. Protection of employees. The legislature shall pass necessary laws for the protection of persons working in mines, factories and other employments dangerous to life or deleterious to health; and fix pains and penalties for the enforcement of the same.

Section 36. When bills must be introduced. No bill shall be considered in either house unless the time of its introduction shall have been at least ten days before the final adjournment of the legislature, unless the legislature shall otherwise direct by a vote of two-thirds of all the members elected to each house, said vote to be taken by yeas and nays and entered upon the journal, or unless the same be at a special session.

Section 37. Revision or amendment. No act shall ever be revised or amended by mere reference to its title, but the act revised or the section amended shall be set forth at full length.

Section 38. Limitation on amendments. No amendment to any bill shall be allowed which shall change the scope and object of the bill.

Section 39. Free transportation to public officer prohibited. It shall not be lawful for any person holding public office in this state to accept or use a pass or to purchase transportation from any railroad or other corporation, other than as the same may be purchased by the general public, and the legislature shall pass laws to enforce this provision.

Section 40. Highway funds. All fees collected by the State of Washington as license fees for motor vehicles and all excise taxes collected by the State of Washington on the sale, distribution or use of motor vehicle fuel and all other state revenue intended to be used for highway purposes, shall be paid into the state treasury and placed in a special fund to be used exclusively for highway purposes. Such highway purposes shall be construed to include the following:

(a) The necessary operating, engineering and legal expenses connected with the administration of public highways, county roads and city streets;

(b) The construction, reconstruction, maintenance, repair, and betterment of public highways, county roads, bridges and city streets; including the cost and expense of (1) acquisition of rights-of-way, (2) installing, maintaining and operating traffic signs and signal lights, (3) policing by the state of public highways, (4) operation of movable span bridges, (5) operation of ferries which are a part of any public highway, county road, or city street;

(c) The payment or refunding of any obligation of the State of Washington, or any political subdivision thereof, for which any of the revenues described in section 1 may have been legally pledged prior to the effective date of this act;

(d) Refunds authorized by law for taxes paid on motor vehicle fuels;

(e) The cost of collection of any revenues described in this section:

Provided, That this section shall not be construed to include revenue from general or special taxes or excises not levied primarily for highway purposes, or apply to vehicle operator's license fees or any excise tax imposed on motor vehicles or the use thereof in lieu of a property tax thereon, or fees for certificates of ownership of motor vehicles. [Amendment 18, 1943 House Joint Resolution No. 4, p 938. Approved November, 1944.]

Section 41. Laws, effective date, initiative, referendum – Amendment or repeal. No act, law, or bill subject to referendum shall take effect until ninety days after the adjournment of the session at which it was enacted. No act, law or bill approved by a majority of the electors voting thereon shall be amended or repealed by the legislature within a period of two years following such enactment: *Provided,* That any such act, law or bill may be amended within two years after such enactment at any regular or special session of the legislature by a vote of two-thirds of all the members elected to each house with full compliance with section 12, Article III, of the Washington Constitution, and no amendatory law adopted in accordance with this provision shall be subject to referendum. But such enactment may be amended or repealed at any general regular or special election by direct vote of the people thereon. These provisions supersede the provisions of subsection (c) of section 1 of this article as amended by the seventh amendment to the Constitution of this state. [Amendment 26, 1951 Substitute Senate Joint Resolution No. 7, p 959. Approved November 4, 1952.]

Section 42. Governmental continuity during emergency periods. The legislature, in order to insure continuity of state and local governmental operations in periods of emergency resulting from enemy attack, shall have the power and the duty, immediately upon and after adoption of this amendment, to enact legislation providing for prompt and temporary succession to the powers and duties of public offices of whatever nature and whether filled by election or appointment, the incumbents and legal successors of which may become unavailable for carrying on the powers and duties of such offices; the legislature shall likewise enact such other measures as may be necessary and proper for insuring the continuity of governmental operations during such emergencies. Legislation enacted under the powers conferred by this amendment shall in all respects conform to the remainder of the Constitution: *Provided,* That if, in the judgment of the legislature at the time of disaster, conformance to the provisions of the Constitution would be impracticable or would admit of undue delay, such legislation may depart during the period of emergency caused by enemy attack only, from the following sections of the Constitution:

Article 14, Sections 1 and 2, Seat of Government;

Article 2, Sections 8, 15 (Amendments 13 and 32), and 22, Membership, Quorum of Legislature and Passage of Bills;

Article 3, Section 10 (Amendment 6), Succession to Governorship: *Provided,* That the legislature shall not depart from Section 10, Article III, as amended by Amendment 6, of the state Constitution relating to the Governor's office so long as any successor therein named is available and capable of assuming the powers and duties of such office as therein prescribed;

Article 3, Section 13, Vacancies in State Offices;

Article 11, Section 6, Vacancies in County Offices;

Article 11, Section 2, Seat of County Government;

Article 3, Section 24, State Records. [Amendment
39, 1961 House Joint Resolution No. 9, p 2758.
Approved November, 1962.]

Section 43. Redistricting. (1) In January of each year
ending in one, a commission shall be established to provide
for the redistricting of state legislative and congressional
districts.

(2) The commission shall be composed of five
members to be selected as follows: The legislative
leader of the two largest political parties in each house
of the legislature shall appoint one voting member to
the commission by January 15th of each year ending in
one. By January 31st of each year ending in one, the four
appointed members, by an affirmative vote of at least
three, shall appoint the remaining member. The fifth
member of the commission, who shall be nonvoting, shall
act as its chairperson. If any appointing authority fails to
make the required appointment by the date established
by this subsection, within five days after that date the
supreme court shall make the required appointment.

(3) No elected official and no person elected to
legislative district, county, or state political party office
may serve on the commission. A commission member shall
not have been an elected official and shall not have been
an elected legislative district, county, or state political
party officer within two years of his or her appointment to
the commission. The provisions of this subsection do not
apply to the office of precinct committee person.

(4) The legislature shall enact laws providing for the implementation of this section, to include additional qualifications for commissioners and additional standards to govern the commission. The legislature shall appropriate funds to enable the commission to carry out its duties.

(5) Each district shall contain a population, excluding nonresident military personnel, as nearly equal as practicable to the population of any other district. To the extent reasonable, each district shall contain contiguous territory, shall be compact and convenient, and shall be separated from adjoining districts by natural geographic barriers, artificial barriers, or political subdivision boundaries. The commission's plan shall not provide for a number of legislative districts different than that established by the legislature. The commission's plan shall not be drawn purposely to favor or discriminate against any political party or group.

(6) The commission shall complete redistricting as soon as possible following the federal decennial census, but no later than January 1st of each year ending in two. At least three of the voting members shall approve such a redistricting plan. If three of the voting members of the commission fail to approve a plan within the time limitations provided in this subsection, the supreme court shall adopt a plan by April 30th of the year ending in two in conformance with the standards set forth in subsection (5) of this section.

(7) The legislature may amend the redistricting plan but must do so by a two-thirds vote of the legislators

elected or appointed to each house of the legislature. Any amendment must have passed both houses by the end of the thirtieth day of the first session convened after the commission has submitted its plan to the legislature. After that day, the plan, with any legislative amendments, constitutes the state districting law.

(8) The legislature shall enact laws providing for the reconvening of a commission for the purpose of modifying a districting law adopted under this section. Such reconvening requires a two-thirds vote of the legislators elected or appointed to each house of the legislature. The commission shall conform to the standards prescribed under subsection (5) of this section and any other standards or procedures that the legislature may provide by law. At least three of the voting members shall approve such a modification. Any modification adopted by the commission may be amended by a two-thirds vote of the legislators elected and appointed to each house of the legislature. The state districting law shall include the modifications with amendments, if any.

(9) The legislature shall prescribe by law the terms of commission members and the method of filling vacancies on the commission.

(10) The supreme court has original jurisdiction to hear and decide all cases involving congressional and legislative redistricting.

(11) Legislative and congressional districts may not be changed or established except pursuant to this section. A districting plan and any legislative amendments to

the plan are not subject to Article III, section 12 of this Constitution. [Amendment 74, 1983 Substitute Senate Joint Resolution No. 103, p 2202. Approved November 8, 1983.]

Article III
The Executive

Section 1. Executive department. The executive department shall consist of a governor, lieutenant governor, secretary of state, treasurer, auditor, attorney general, superintendent of public instruction, and a commissioner of public lands, who shall be severally chosen by the qualified electors of the state at the same time and place of voting as for the members of the legislature.

Section 2. Governor, term of office. The supreme executive power of this state shall be vested in a governor, who shall hold his office for a term of four years, and until his successor is elected and qualified.

Section 3. Other executive officers, terms of office. The lieutenant governor, secretary of state, treasurer, auditor, attorney general, superintendent of public instruction, and commissioner of public lands, shall hold their offices for four years respectively, and until their successors are elected and qualified.

Section 4. Returns of elections, canvass, etc. The returns of every election for the officers named in the first section of this article shall be sealed up and transmitted to the seat of government by the returning officers, directed to the secretary of state, who shall deliver the same to the speaker of the house of representatives at the first meeting of the house thereafter, who shall open, publish and declare the result thereof in the presence of a majority of the members of both houses. The person having the highest number of votes shall be declared duly elected, and a certificate thereof shall be given to such person, signed by the presiding officers of both houses; but if any two or more shall be highest and equal in votes for the same office, one of them shall be chosen by the joint vote of both houses. Contested elections for such officers shall be decided by the legislature in such manner as shall be determined by law. The terms of all officers named in section one of this article shall commence on the second Monday in January after their election until otherwise provided by law.

Section 5. General duties of governor. The governor may require information in writing from the officers of the state upon any subject relating to the duties of their respective offices, and shall see that the laws are faithfully executed.

Section 6. Messages. He shall communicate at every session by message to the legislature the condition of the affairs of the state, and recommend such measures as he shall deem expedient for their action.

Section 7. Extra legislative sessions. He may, on extraordinary occasions, convene the legislature by proclamation, in which shall be stated the purposes for which the legislature is convened.

Section 8. Commander-in-chief. He shall be commander-in-chief of the military in the state except when they shall be called into the service of the United States.

Section 9. Pardoning power. The pardoning power shall be vested in the governor under such regulations and restrictions as may be prescribed by law.

Section 10. Vacancy in office of governor. In case of the removal, resignation, death or disability of the governor, the duties of the office shall devolve upon the lieutenant governor; and in case of a vacancy in both the offices of governor and lieutenant governor, the duties of the governor shall devolve upon the secretary of state. In addition to the line of succession to the office and duties of governor as hereinabove indicated, if the necessity shall arise, in order to fill the vacancy in the office of governor, the following state officers shall succeed to the duties of governor and in the order named, viz.: Treasurer, auditor, attorney general, superintendent of public instruction and commissioner of public lands. In case of the death, disability, failure or refusal of the person regularly elected to the office of governor to qualify at the time provided by law, the duties of the office shall devolve upon the person regularly elected to and qualified for the office of lieutenant governor, who shall act as governor until the disability be removed, or a governor be elected; and in case of the death, disability, failure or refusal of both the governor and the lieutenant governor elect to qualify, the duties of the governor shall devolve upon the secretary of state; and in addition to the line of succession to the office and duties of governor as hereinabove indicated, if there shall be the failure or refusal of any officer named above to qualify, and if the necessity shall arise by reason thereof, then in that event in order to fill the vacancy in the office of governor, the following state officers shall succeed to the duties of governor in the order named, viz: Treasurer, auditor, attorney general, superintendent of public instruction and commissioner of public lands. Any person succeeding to the office of governor as in this section provided, shall perform the duties of such office only until the disability be removed, or a governor be elected and qualified; and if a vacancy occur more than thirty days before the next general election occurring within two years after the commencement of the term, a person shall be elected at such election to fill the office of governor for the remainder of the unexpired term. [Amendment 6, 1909 p 642 Section 1. Approved November, 1910.]

Section 11. Remission of fines and forfeitures. The governor shall have power to remit fines and forfeitures, under such regulations as may be prescribed by law, and shall report to the legislature at its next meeting each case of reprieve, commutation or pardon granted, and the reasons for granting the same, and also the names of all persons in whose favor remission of fines and forfeitures shall have been made, and the several amounts remitted and the reasons for the remission.

Section 12. Veto powers. Every act which shall have passed the legislature shall be, before it becomes a law, presented to the governor. If he approves, he shall sign it; but if not, he shall return it, with his objections, to that house in which it shall have originated, which house shall enter the objections at large upon the journal and proceed to reconsider. If, after such reconsideration, two-thirds of the members present shall agree to pass the bill it shall be sent, together with the objections, to the other house, by which it shall likewise be reconsidered, and if approved by two-thirds of the members present, it shall become a law; but in all such cases the vote of both houses shall be determined by the yeas and nays, and the names of the members voting for or against the bill shall be entered upon the journal of each house respectively. If any bill shall not be returned by the governor within five days, Sundays excepted, after it shall be presented to him, it shall become a law without his signature, unless the general adjournment shall prevent its return, in which case it shall become a law unless the governor, within twenty days next after the adjournment, Sundays excepted, shall file such bill with his objections thereto, in the office of secretary of state, who shall lay the same before the legislature at its next session in like manner as if it had been returned by the governor: *Provided,* That within forty-five days next after the adjournment, Sundays excepted, the legislature may, upon petition by a two-thirds majority or more of the membership of each house, reconvene in extraordinary session, not to exceed five days duration, solely to reconsider any bills vetoed. If any bill presented to the governor contain several sections or appropriation items, he may object to one or more sections or appropriation items while approving other portions of the bill: *Provided,* That he may not object to less than an entire section, except that if the section contain one or more appropriation items he may object to any such appropriation item or items. In case of objection he shall append to the bill, at the time of signing it, a statement of the section or sections, appropriation item or items to which he objects and the reasons therefor; and the section or sections, appropriation item or items so objected to shall not take effect unless passed over the governor's objection, as hereinbefore provided. The provisions of Article II, section 12 insofar as they are inconsistent herewith are hereby repealed. [Amendment 62, 1974 Senate Joint Resolution No. 140, p 806. Approved November 5, 1974.]

Section 13. Vacancy in appointive office. When, during a recess of the legislature, a vacancy shall happen in any office, the appointment to which is vested in the legislature, or when at any time a vacancy shall have occurred in any other state office, for the filling of which vacancy no provision is made elsewhere in this Constitution, the governor shall fill such vacancy by appointment, which shall expire when a successor shall have been elected and qualified.

Section 14. Salary. The governor shall receive an annual salary of four thousand dollars, which may be increased by law, but shall never exceed six thousand dollars per annum.

Section 15. Commissions, how issued. All commissions shall issue in the name of the state, shall be signed by the governor, sealed with the seal of the state, and attested by the secretary of state.

Section 16. Lieutenant governor, duties and salary. The lieutenant governor shall be presiding officer of the state senate, and shall discharge such other duties as may be prescribed by law. He shall receive an annual salary of one thousand dollars, which may be increased by the legislature, but shall never exceed three thousand dollars per annum.

Section 17. Secretary of state, duties and salary. The secretary of state shall keep a record of the official acts of the legislature, and executive department of the state, and shall, when required, lay the same, and all matters relative thereto, before either branch of the legislature, and shall perform such other duties as shall be assigned him by law. He shall receive an annual salary of twenty-five hundred dollars, which may be increased by the legislature, but shall never exceed three thousand dollars per annum.

Section 18. Seal. There shall be a seal of the state kept by the secretary of state for official purposes, which shall be called, "The Seal of the State of Washington."

Section 19. State treasurer, duties and salary. The treasurer shall perform such duties as shall be prescribed by law. He shall receive an annual salary of two thousand dollars, which may be increased by the legislature, but shall never exceed four thousand dollars per annum.

Section 20. State auditor, duties and salary. The auditor shall be auditor of public accounts, and shall have such powers and perform such duties in connection therewith as may be prescribed by law. He shall receive an annual salary of two thousand dollars, which may be increased by the legislature, but shall never exceed three thousand dollars per annum.

Section 21. Attorney general, duties and salary. The attorney general shall be the legal adviser of the state officers, and shall perform such other duties as may be prescribed by law. He shall receive an annual salary of two thousand dollars, which may be increased by the legislature, but shall never exceed thirty-five hundred dollars per annum.

Section 22. Superintendent of public instruction, duties and salary. The superintendent of public instruction shall have supervision over all matters pertaining to public schools, and shall perform such specific duties as may be prescribed by law. He shall receive an annual salary of twenty-five hundred dollars, which may be increased by law, but shall never exceed four thousand dollars per annum.

Section 23. Commissioner of public lands – Compensation. The commissioner of public lands shall perform such duties and receive such compensation as the legislature may direct.

Section 24. Records, where kept, etc. The governor, secretary of state, treasurer, auditor, superintendent of public instruction, commissioner of public lands and attorney general shall severally keep the public records, books and papers relating to their respective offices, at the seat of government, at which place also the governor, secretary of state, treasurer and auditor shall reside.

Section 25. Qualifications, compensation, offices which may be abolished. No person, except a citizen of the United States and a qualified elector of this state, shall be eligible to hold any state office. The compensation for state officers shall not be increased or diminished during the term for which they shall have been elected. The legislature may in its discretion abolish the offices of the lieutenant governor, auditor and commissioner of public lands. [Amendment 31, 1955 Senate Joint Resolution No. 6, p 1861. Approved November 6, 1956.]

Article IV
The Judiciary

Section 1. Judicial power, where vested. The judicial power of the state shall be vested in a supreme court, superior courts, justices of the peace, and such inferior courts as the legislature may provide.

Section 2. Supreme court. The supreme court shall consist of five judges, a majority of whom shall be necessary to form a quorum, and pronounce a decision. The said court shall always be open for the transaction of business except on nonjudicial days. In the determination of causes all decisions of the court shall be given in writing and the grounds of the decision shall be stated. The legislature may increase the number of judges of the supreme court from time to time and may provide for separate departments of said court.

Section 2(a). Temporary performance of judicial duties. When necessary for the prompt and orderly administration of justice a majority of the Supreme Court is empowered to authorize judges or retired judges of courts of record of this state, to perform, temporarily, judicial duties in the Supreme Court, and to authorize any superior court judge to perform judicial duties in any superior court of this state. [Amendment 38, 1961 House Joint Resolution No. 6, p 2757. Approved November, 1962.]

Section 3. Election and terms of supreme court judges. The judges of the supreme court shall be elected by the qualified electors of the state at large at the general state election at the times and places at which state officers are elected, unless some other time be provided by the legislature. The first election of judges of the supreme court shall be at the election which shall be held upon the adoption of this Constitution and the judges elected thereat shall be classified by lot, so that two shall hold their office for the term of three years, two for the term of five years, and one for the term of seven years. The lot shall be drawn by the judges who shall for that purpose assemble at the seat of government, and they shall cause the result thereof to be certified to the secretary of state, and filed in his office. The supreme court shall select a chief justice from its own membership to serve for a four-year term at the pleasure of a majority of the court as prescribed by supreme court rule. The chief justice shall preside at all sessions of the supreme court. In case of the absence of the chief justice, the majority of the remaining court shall select one of their members to serve as acting chief justice. After the first election the terms of judges elected shall be six years from and after the second Monday in January next succeeding their election. If a vacancy occur in the office of a judge of the supreme court the governor shall only appoint a person to ensure the number of judges as specified by the legislature, to hold the office until the election and qualification of a judge to fill the vacancy, which election shall take place at the next succeeding general election, and the judge so elected shall hold the office for the remainder of the unexpired term. The term of office of the judges of the supreme court, first elected, shall commence as soon as the state shall have been admitted into the Union, and continue for the term herein provided, and until their successors are elected and qualified. The sessions of the supreme court shall be held at the seat of government until otherwise provided by law. [Amendment 89, 1995 Substitute Senate Joint Resolution No. 8210, p 2905. Approved November 7, 1995.]

Section 3(a). Retirement of supreme court and superior court judges. A judge of the supreme court or the superior court shall retire from judicial office at the end of the calendar year in which he attains the age of seventy-five years. The legislature may, from time to time, fix a lesser age for mandatory retirement, not earlier than the end of the calendar year in which any such judge attains the age of seventy years, as the legislature deems proper. This provision shall not affect the term to which any such judge shall have been elected or appointed prior to, or at the time of, approval and ratification of this provision. Notwithstanding the limitations of this section, the legislature may by general law authorize or require the retirement of judges for physical or mental disability, or any cause rendering judges incapable of performing their judicial duties. [Amendment 25, 1951 House Joint Resolution No. 6, p 960. Approved November 4, 1952.]

Section 4. Jurisdiction. The supreme court shall have original jurisdiction in habeas corpus, and quo warranto and mandamus as to all state officers, and appellate jurisdiction in all actions and proceedings, excepting that its appellate jurisdiction shall not extend to civil actions at law for the recovery of money or personal property when the original amount in controversy, or the value of the property does not exceed the sum of two hundred dollars ($200) unless the action involves the legality of a tax, impost, assessment, toll, municipal fine, or the validity of a statute. The supreme court shall also have power to issue writs of mandamus, review, prohibition, habeas corpus, certiorari and all other writs necessary and proper to the complete exercise of its appellate and revisory jurisdiction. Each of the judges shall have power to issue writs of habeas corpus to any part of the state upon petition by or on behalf of any person held in actual custody, and may make such writs returnable before himself, or before the supreme court, or before any superior court of the state or any judge thereof.

Section 5. Superior court – Election of judges, terms of, etc. There shall be in each of the organized counties of this state a superior court for which at least one judge shall be elected by the qualified electors of the county at the general state election: **Provided,** That until otherwise directed by the legislature one judge only shall be elected for the counties of Spokane and Stevens; one judge for the county of Whitman; one judge for the counties of Lincoln, Okanogan, Douglas and Adams; one judge for the counties of Walla Walla and Franklin; one judge for the counties of Columbia, Garfield and Asotin; one judge for the counties of Kittitas, Yakima and Klickitat; one judge for the counties of Clarke, Skamania, Pacific, Cowlitz and Wahkiakum; one judge for the counties of Thurston, Chehalis, Mason and Lewis; one judge for the county of Pierce; one judge for the county of King; one judge for the counties of Jefferson, Island, Kitsap, San Juan and Clallam; and one judge for the counties of Whatcom, Skagit and Snohomish. In any county where there shall be more than one superior judge, there may be as many sessions of the superior court at the same time as there are judges thereof, and whenever the governor shall direct a superior judge to hold court in any county other than that for which he has been elected, there may be as many sessions of the superior court in said county at the same time as there are judges therein or assigned to duty therein by the governor, and the business of the court shall be so distributed and assigned by law or in the absence of legislation therefor, by such rules and orders of court as shall best promote and secure the convenient and expeditious transaction thereof. The judgments, decrees, orders and proceedings of any session of the superior court held by any one or more of the judges of such court shall be equally effectual as if all the judges of said court presided at such session. The first superior judges elected under this Constitution shall hold their offices for the period of three years, and until their successors shall be elected and qualified, and thereafter the term of office of all superior judges in this state shall be for four years from the second Monday in January next succeeding their election and until their successors are elected and qualified. The first election of judges of the superior court shall be at the election held for the adoption of this Constitution. If a vacancy occurs in the office of judge of the superior court, the governor shall appoint a person to hold the office until the election and qualification of a judge to fill the vacancy, which election shall be at the next succeeding general election, and the judge so elected shall hold office for the remainder of the unexpired term.

Section 6. Jurisdiction of superior courts. Superior courts and district courts have concurrent jurisdiction in cases in equity. The superior court shall have original jurisdiction in all cases at law which involve the title or possession of real property, or the legality of any tax, impost, assessment, toll, or municipal fine, and in all other cases in which the demand or the value of the property in controversy amounts to three thousand dollars or as otherwise determined by law, or a lesser sum in excess of the jurisdiction granted to justices of the peace and other inferior courts, and in all criminal cases amounting to felony, and in all cases of misdemeanor not otherwise provided for by law; of actions of forcible entry and detainer; of proceedings in insolvency; of actions to prevent or abate a nuisance; of all matters of probate, of divorce, and for annulment of marriage; and for such special cases and proceedings as are not otherwise provided for. The superior court shall also have original jurisdiction in all cases and of all proceedings in which jurisdiction shall not have been by law vested exclusively in some other court; and said court shall have the power of naturalization and to issue papers therefor. They shall have such appellate jurisdiction in cases arising in justices' and other inferior courts in their respective counties as may be prescribed by law. They shall always be open, except on nonjudicial days, and their process shall extend to all parts of the state. Said courts and their judges shall have power to issue writs of mandamus, quo warranto, review, certiorari, prohibition, and writs of habeas corpus, on petition by or on behalf of any person in actual custody in their respective counties. Injunctions and writs of prohibition and of habeas corpus may be issued and served on legal holidays and nonjudicial days. [Amendment 87, 1993 House Joint Resolution No. 4201, p 3063. Approved November 2, 1993.]

Section 7. Exchange of judges - judge pro tempore. The judge of any superior court may hold a superior court in any county at the request of the judge of the superior court thereof, and upon the request of the governor it shall be his or her duty to do so. A case in the superior court may be tried by a judge pro tempore either with the agreement of the parties if the judge pro tempore is a member of the bar, is agreed upon in writing by the parties litigant or their attorneys of record, and is approved by the court and sworn to try the case; or without the agreement of the parties if the judge pro tempore is a sitting elected judge and is acting as a judge pro tempore pursuant to supreme court rule. The supreme court rule must require assignments of judges pro tempore based on the judges' experience and must provide for the right, exercisable once during a case, to a change of judge pro tempore. Such right shall be in addition to any other right provided by law. However, if a previously elected judge of the superior court retires leaving a pending case in which the judge has made discretionary rulings, the judge is entitled to hear the pending case as a judge pro tempore without any written agreement. [Amendment 94, 2001 Engrossed

Senate Joint Resolution No. 8208, p 2327. Approved November 6, 2001.]

Section 8. Absence of judicial officer. Any judicial officer who shall absent himself from the state for more than sixty consecutive days shall be deemed to have forfeited his office: *Provided,* That in cases of extreme necessity the governor may extend the leave of absence such time as the necessity therefor shall exist.

Section 9. Removal of judges, attorney general, etc. Any judge of any court of record, the attorney general, or any prosecuting attorney may be removed from office by joint resolution of the legislature, in which three-fourths of the members elected to each house shall concur, for incompetency, corruption, malfeasance, or delinquency in office, or other sufficient cause stated in such resolution. But no removal shall be made unless the officer complained of shall have been served with a copy of the charges against him as the ground of removal, and shall have an opportunity of being heard in his defense. Such resolution shall be entered at length on the journal of both houses and on the question of removal the ayes and nays shall also be entered on the journal.

Section 10. Justices of the peace. The legislature shall determine the number of justices of the peace to be elected and shall prescribe by law the powers, duties and jurisdiction of justices of the peace: *Provided,* That such jurisdiction granted by the legislature shall not trench upon the jurisdiction of superior or other courts of record, except that justices of the peace may be made police justices of incorporated cities and towns. Justices of the peace shall have original jurisdiction in cases where the demand or value of the property in controversy is less than three hundred dollars or such greater sum, not to exceed three thousand dollars or as otherwise determined by law, as shall be prescribed by the legislature. In incorporated cities or towns having more than five thousand inhabitants, the justices of the peace shall receive such salary as may be provided by law, and shall receive no fees for their own use. [Amendment 65, part, 1977 Senate Joint Resolution No. 113, p 1714. Approved November 8, 1977.]

Section 11. Courts of record. The supreme court and the superior courts shall be courts of record, and the legislature shall have power to provide that any of the courts of this state, excepting justices of the peace, shall be courts of record.

Section 12. Inferior courts. The legislature shall prescribe by law the jurisdiction and powers of any of the inferior courts which may be established in pursuance of this Constitution.

Section 13. Salaries of judicial officers – How paid, etc. No judicial officer, except court commissioners and unsalaried justices of the peace, shall receive to his own use any fees or perquisites of office. The judges of the supreme court and judges of the superior courts shall severally at stated times, during their continuance in office, receive for their services the salaries prescribed by law therefor, which shall not be increased after their election, nor during the term for which they shall have been elected. The salaries of the judges of the supreme court shall be paid by the state. One-half of the salary of each of the superior court judges shall be paid by the state, and the other one-half by the county or counties for which he is elected. In cases where a judge is provided for more than one county, that portion of his salary which is to be paid by the counties shall be apportioned between or among them according to the assessed value of their taxable property, to be determined by the assessment next preceding the time for which such salary is to be paid.

Section 14. Salaries of supreme and superior court judges. Each of the judges of the supreme court shall receive an annual salary of four thousand dollars ($4,000); each of the superior court judges shall receive an annual salary of three thousand dollars ($3,000), which said salaries shall be payable quarterly. The legislature may increase the salaries of judges herein provided.

Section 15. Ineligibility of judges. The judges of the supreme court and the judges of the superior court shall be ineligible to any other office or public employment than a judicial office, or employment, during the term for which they shall have been elected.

Section 16. Charging juries. Judges shall not charge juries with respect to matters of fact, nor comment thereon, but shall declare the law.

Section 17. Eligibility of judges. No person shall be eligible to the office of judge of the supreme court, or judge of a superior court, unless he shall have been admitted to practice in the courts of record of this state, or of the Territory of Washington.

Section 18. Supreme court reporter. The judges of the supreme court shall appoint a reporter for the decisions of that court, who shall be removable at their pleasure. He shall receive such annual salary as shall be prescribed by law.

Section 19. Judges may not practice law. No judge of a court of record shall practice law in any court of this state during his continuance in office.

Section 20. Decisions, when to be made. Every cause submitted to a judge of a superior court for his decision shall be decided by him within ninety days from the submission thereof; *Provided,* That if within said period of ninety days a rehearing shall have been ordered, then the period within which he is to decide shall commence at the time the cause is submitted upon such a hearing.

Section 21. Publication of opinions. The legislature shall provide for the speedy publication of opinions of the supreme court, and all opinions shall be free for publication by any person.

Section 22. Clerk of the supreme court. The judges of the supreme court shall appoint a clerk of that court who shall be removable at their pleasure, but the legislature may provide for the election of the clerk of the supreme court, and prescribe the term of his office. The clerk of the supreme court shall receive such compensation by salary only as shall be provided by law.

Section 23. Court commissioners. There may be appointed in each county, by the judge of the superior court having jurisdiction therein, one or more court commissioners, not exceeding three in number, who shall have authority to perform like duties as a judge of the superior court at chambers, subject to revision by such judge, to take depositions and to perform such other business connected with the administration of justice as may be prescribed by law.

Section 24. Rules for superior courts. The judges of the superior courts, shall from time to time, establish uniform rules for the government of the superior courts.

Section 25. Reports of superior court judges. Superior judges, shall on or before the first day of November in each year, report in writing to the judges of the supreme court such defects and omissions in the laws as their experience may suggest, and the judges of the supreme court shall on or before the first day of January in each year report in writing to the governor such defects and omissions in the laws as they may believe to exist.

Section 26. Clerk of the superior court. The county clerk shall be by virtue of his office, clerk of the superior court.

Section 27. Style of process. The style of all process shall be, "The State of Washington," and all prosecutions shall be conducted in its name and by its authority.

Section 28. Oath of judges. Every judge of the supreme court, and every judge of a superior court shall, before entering upon the duties of his office, take and subscribe an oath that he will support the Constitution of the United States and the Constitution of the State of Washington, and will faithfully and impartially discharge the duties of judge to the best of his ability, which oath shall be filed in the office of the secretary of state.

Section 29. Election of superior court judges. Notwithstanding any provision of this Constitution to the contrary, if, after the last day as provided by law for the withdrawal of declarations of candidacy has expired, only one candidate has filed for any single position of superior court judge in any county containing a population of one hundred thousand or more, no primary or election shall be held as to such position, and a certificate of election shall be issued to such candidate. If, after any contested primary for superior court judge in any county, only one candidate is entitled to have his name printed on the general election ballot for any single position, no election shall be held as to such position, and a certificate of election shall be issued to such candidate: *Provided,* That in the event that there is filed with the county auditor within ten days after the date of the primary, a petition indicating that a write in campaign will be conducted for such single position and signed by one hundred registered voters qualified to vote with respect of the office, then such single position shall be subject to the general election. Provisions for the contingency of the death or disqualification of a sole candidate between the last date for withdrawal and the time when the election would be held but for the provisions of this section, and such other provisions as may be deemed necessary to implement the provisions of this section, may be enacted by the legislature. [Amendment 41, 1965 ex.s. Substitute Senate Joint Resolution No. 6, p 2815. Approved November 8, 1966.]

Section 30. Court of appeals. (1) *Authorization.* In addition to the courts authorized in section 1 of this article, judicial power is vested in a court of appeals, which shall be established by statute.

(2) *Jurisdiction.* The jurisdiction of the court

of appeals shall be as provided by statute or by rules authorized by statute.

(3) *Review of Superior Court.* Superior court actions may be reviewed by the court of appeals or by the supreme court as provided by statute or by rule authorized by statute.

(4) *Judges.* The number, manner of election, compensation, terms of office, removal and retirement of judges of the court of appeals shall be as provided by statute.

(5) *Administration and Procedure.* The administration and procedures of the court of appeals shall be as provided by rules issued by the supreme court.

(6) *Conflicts.* The provisions of this section shall supersede any conflicting provisions in prior sections of this article. [Amendment 50, 1967 Senate Joint Resolution No. 6; see 1969 p 2975. Approved November 5, 1968.]

Section 31. Commission on judicial conduct. (1) There shall be a commission on judicial conduct, existing as an independent agency of the judicial branch, and consisting of a judge selected by and from the court of appeals judges, a judge selected by and from the superior court judges, a judge selected by and from the limited jurisdiction court judges, two persons admitted to the practice of law in this state selected by the state bar association, and six persons who are not attorneys appointed by the governor.

(2) Whenever the commission receives a complaint against a judge or justice, or otherwise has reason to be-

lieve that a judge or justice should be admonished, reprimanded, censured, suspended, removed, or retired, the commission shall first investigate the complaint or belief and then conduct initial proceedings for the purpose of determining whether probable cause exists for conducting a public hearing or hearings to deal with the complaint or belief. The investigation and initial proceedings shall be confidential. Upon beginning an initial proceeding, the commission shall notify the judge or justice of the existence of and basis for the initial proceeding.

(3) Whenever the commission concludes, based on an initial proceeding, that there is probable cause to believe that a judge or justice has violated a rule of judicial conduct or that the judge or justice suffers from a disability which is permanent or likely to become permanent and which seriously interferes with the performance of judicial duties, the commission shall conduct a public hearing or hearings and shall make public all those records of the initial proceeding that provide the basis for its conclusion. If the commission concludes that there is not probable cause, it shall notify the judge or justice of its conclusion.

(4) Upon the completion of the hearing or hearings, the commission in open session shall either dismiss the case, or shall admonish, reprimand, or censure the judge or justice, or shall censure the judge or justice and recommend to the supreme court the suspension or removal of the judge or justice, or shall recommend to the supreme court the retirement of the judge or justice. The commission may not recommend suspension or removal unless it

censures the judge or justice for the violation serving as the basis for the recommendation. The commission may recommend retirement of a judge or justice for a disability which is permanent or likely to become permanent and which seriously interferes with the performance of judicial duties.

(5) Upon the recommendation of the commission, the supreme court may suspend, remove, or retire a judge or justice. The office of a judge or justice retired or removed by the supreme court becomes vacant, and that person is ineligible for judicial office until eligibility is reinstated by the supreme court. The salary of a removed judge or justice shall cease. The supreme court shall specify the effect upon salary when it suspends a judge or justice. The supreme court may not suspend, remove, or retire a judge or justice until the commission, after notice and hearing, recommends that action be taken, and the supreme court conducts a hearing, after notice, to review commission proceedings and findings against the judge or justice.

(6) Within thirty days after the commission admonishes, reprimands, or censures a judge or justice, the judge or justice shall have a right of appeal de novo to the supreme court.

(7) Any matter before the commission or supreme court may be disposed of by a stipulation entered into in a public proceeding. The stipulation shall be signed by the judge or justice and the commission or court. The stipulation may impose any terms and conditions deemed appro-

priate by the commission or court. A stipulation shall set forth all material facts relating to the proceeding and the conduct of the judge or justice.

(8) Whenever the commission adopts a recommendation that a judge or justice be removed, the judge or justice shall be suspended immediately, with salary, from his or her judicial position until a final determination is made by the supreme court.

(9) The legislature shall provide for commissioners' terms of office and compensation. The commission shall employ one or more investigative officers with appropriate professional training and experience. The investigative officers of the commission shall report directly to the commission. The commission shall also employ such administrative or other staff as are necessary to manage the affairs of the commission.

(10) The commission shall, to the extent that compliance does not conflict with this section, comply with laws of general applicability to state agencies with respect to rule-making procedures, and with respect to public notice of and attendance at commission proceedings other than initial proceedings. The commission shall establish rules of procedure for commission proceedings including due process and confidentiality of proceedings. [**Amendment 97,** 2005 Senate Joint Resolution No. 8207, pp 2799, 2800. Approved November 8, 2005.]

✤ ✤ ✤

Article V
Impeachment

Section 1. Impeachment – Power of and procedure.
The house of representatives shall have the sole power
of impeachment. The concurrence of a majority of all
the members shall be necessary to an impeachment. All
impeachments shall be tried by the senate, and, when
sitting for that purpose, the senators shall be upon oath
or affirmation to do justice according to law and evidence.
When the governor or lieutenant governor is on trial, the
chief justice of the supreme court shall preside. No person
shall be convicted without a concurrence of two-thirds of
the senators elected.

Section 2. Officers liable to. The governor and other
state and judicial officers, except judges and justices of
courts not of record, shall be liable to impeachment for
high crimes or misdemeanors, or malfeasance in office,
but judgment in such cases shall extend only to removal
from office and disqualification to hold any office of honor,
trust or profit, in the state. The party, whether convicted
or acquitted, shall, nevertheless, be liable to prosecution,
trial, judgment and punishment according to law.

Section 3. Removal from office. All officers not liable to
impeachment shall be subject to removal for misconduct
or malfeasance in office, in such manner as may be
provided by law.

Article VI
Elections and Elective Rights

Section 1. Qualifications of electors. All persons of the age of eighteen years or over who are citizens of the United States and who have lived in the state, county, and precinct thirty days immediately preceding the election at which they offer to vote, except those disqualified by Article VI, section 3 of this Constitution, shall be entitled to vote at all elections. [Amendment 63, 1974 Senate Joint Resolution No. 143, p 807. Approved November 5, 1974.]

Section 1(a). Voter qualifications for presidential elections. In consideration of those citizens of the United States who become residents of the state of Washington during the year of a presidential election with the intention of making this state their permanent residence, this section is for the purpose of authorizing such persons who can meet all qualifications for voting as set forth in section 1 of this article, except for residence, to vote for presidential electors or for the office of President and Vice-President of the United States, as the case may be, but no other: *Provided,* That such persons have resided in the state at least sixty days immediately preceding the presidential election concerned.

The legislature shall establish the time, manner and place for such persons to cast such presidential ballots. [Amendment 46, 1965 ex.s. Substitute House Joint Resolution No. 4, p 2820. Approved November 8, 1966.]

Section 2. School elections – Franchise, how extended.
[This section stricken by Amendment 5, see Art. 6 Section 1.]

Section 3. Who disqualified. All persons convicted of infamous crime unless restored to their civil rights and all persons while they are judicially declared mentally incompetent are excluded from the elective franchise. [Amendment 83, 1988 House Joint Resolution No. 4231, p 1553. Approved November 8, 1988.]

Section 4. Residence, contingencies affecting. For the purpose of voting and eligibility to office no person shall be deemed to have gained a residence by reason of his presence or lost it by reason of his absence, while in the civil or military service of the state or of the United States, nor while a student at any institution of learning, nor while kept at public expense at any poor-house or other asylum, nor while confined in public prison, nor while engaged in the navigation of the waters of this state or of the United States, or of the high seas.

Section 5. Voter – When privileged from arrest. Voters shall in all cases except treason, felony, and breach of the peace be privileged from arrest during their attendance at elections and in going to, and returning therefrom. No elector shall be required to do military duty on the day of any election except in time of war or public danger.

Section 6. Ballot. All elections shall be by ballot. The legislature shall provide for such method of voting as will secure to every elector absolute secrecy in preparing and depositing his ballot.

Section 7. Registration. The legislature shall enact a registration law, and shall require a compliance with such law before any elector shall be allowed to vote; *Provided,* that this provision is not compulsory upon the legislature except as to cities and towns having a population of over five hundred inhabitants. In all other cases the legislature may or may not require registration as a pre-requisite to the right to vote, and the same system of registration need not be adopted for both classes.

Section 8. Elections, time of holding. The first election of county and district officers not otherwise provided for in this Constitution shall be on the Tuesday next after the first Monday in November 1890, and thereafter all elections for such officers shall be held bi-ennially on the Tuesday next succeeding the first Monday in November. The first election of all state officers not otherwise provided for in this Constitution, after the election held for the adoption of this Constitution, shall be on the Tuesday next after the first Monday in November, 1892, and the elections for such state officers shall be held in every fourth year thereafter on the Tuesday succeeding the first Monday in November.

Article VII
Revenue and Taxation

Section 1. Taxation. The power of taxation shall never be suspended, surrendered or contracted away. All taxes shall be uniform upon the same class of property within the territorial limits of the authority levying the tax and shall be levied and collected for public purposes only. The word "property" as used herein shall mean and include everything, whether tangible or intangible, subject to ownership. All real estate shall constitute one class: *Provided,* That the legislature may tax mines and mineral resources and lands devoted to reforestation by either a yield tax or an ad valorem tax at such rate as it may fix, or by both. Such property as the legislature may by general laws provide shall be exempt from taxation. Property of the United States and of the state, counties, school districts and other municipal corporations, and credits secured by property actually taxed in this state, not exceeding in value the value of such property, shall be exempt from taxation. The legislature shall have power, by appropriate legislation, to exempt personal property to the amount of fifteen thousand ($15,000.00) dollars for each head of a family liable to assessment and taxation under the provisions of the laws of this state of which the individual is the actual bona fide owner. [Amendment 98, 2006 House Joint Resolution No. 4223, p 2117. Approved November 7, 2006.]

Section 2. Limitation on levies. Except as hereinafter
provided and notwithstanding any other provision of this
Constitution, the aggregate of all tax levies upon real and
personal property by the state and all taxing districts now
existing or hereafter created, shall not in any year exceed
one percent of the true and fair value of such property
in money. Nothing herein shall prevent levies at the rates
now provided by law by or for any port or public utility
district. The term "taxing district" for the purposes
of this section shall mean any political subdivision,
municipal corporation, district, or other governmental
agency authorized by law to levy, or have levied for it,
ad valorem taxes on property, other than a port or public
utility district. Such aggregate limitation or any specific
limitation imposed by law in conformity therewith may
be exceeded only as follows:

(a) By any taxing district when specifically
authorized so to do by a majority of at least three-fifths of
the voters of the taxing district voting on the proposition
to levy such additional tax submitted not more than
twelve months prior to the date on which the proposed
initial levy is to be made and not oftener than twice in such
twelve month period, either at a special election or at the
regular election of such taxing district, at which election
the number of voters voting "yes" on the proposition shall
constitute three-fifths of a number equal to forty percent
of the total number of voters voting in such taxing district
at the last preceding general election when the number
of voters voting on the proposition does not exceed forty

percent of the total number of voters voting in such taxing district in the last preceding general election; or by a majority of at least three-fifths of the voters of the taxing district voting on the proposition to levy when the number of voters voting on the proposition exceeds forty percent of the number of voters voting in such taxing district in the last preceding general election. Notwithstanding any other provision of this Constitution, any proposition pursuant to this subsection to levy additional tax for the support of the common schools or fire protection districts may provide such support for a period of up to four years and any proposition to levy an additional tax to support the construction, modernization, or remodelling of school facilities or fire facilities may provide such support for a period not exceeding six years. Notwithstanding any other provision of this subsection, a proposition under this subsection to levy an additional tax for a school district shall be authorized by a majority of the voters voting on the proposition, regardless of the number of voters voting on the proposition;

(b) By any taxing district otherwise authorized by law to issue general obligation bonds for capital purposes, for the sole purpose of making the required payments of principal and interest on general obligation bonds issued solely for capital purposes, other than the replacement of equipment, when authorized so to do by majority of at least three-fifths of the voters of the taxing district voting on the proposition to issue such bonds and to pay the principal and interest thereon by annual tax levies in excess of the limitation herein provided during the term of such bonds, submitted not oftener than twice in any calendar year, at an election held in the manner provided by law for bond elections in such taxing district, at which election the total number of voters voting on the proposition shall constitute not less than forty percent of the total number of voters voting in such taxing district at the last preceding general election. Any such taxing district shall have the right by vote of its governing body to refund any general obligation bonds of said district issued for capital purposes only, and to provide for the interest thereon and amortization thereof by annual levies in excess of the tax limitation provided for herein. The provisions of this section shall also be subject to the limitations contained in Article VIII, Section 6, of this Constitution;

(c) By the state or any taxing district for the purpose of preventing the impairment of the obligation of a contract when ordered so to do by a court of last resort. [Amendment 101, 2007 Engrossed House Joint Resolution No. 4204, pp 3143-3145. Approved November 6, 2007.]

Section 3. Taxation of federal agencies and property. The United States and its agencies and instrumentalities, and their property, may be taxed under any of the tax laws of this state, whenever and in such manner as such taxation may be authorized or permitted under the laws of the United States, notwithstanding anything to the contrary in the Constitution of this state. [Amendment 19, 1945 House Joint Resolution No. 9, p 932. Approved November, 1946.]

Section 4. No surrender of power or suspension of tax on corporate property. [Stricken by Amendment 14. Set out following Art. 7 Section 1, above.]

Section 5. Taxes, how levied. No tax shall be levied except in pursuance of law; and every law imposing a tax shall state distinctly the object of the same to which only it shall be applied.

Section 6. Taxes, how paid. All taxes levied and collected for state purposes shall be paid in money only into the state treasury.

Section 7. Annual statement. An accurate statement of the receipts and expenditures of the public moneys shall be published annually in such manner as the legislature may provide.

Section 8. Tax to cover deficiencies. Whenever the expenses of any fiscal year shall exceed the income, the legislature may provide for levying a tax for the ensuing fiscal year, sufficient, with other sources of income, to pay the deficiency, as well as the estimated expenses of the ensuing fiscal year.

Section 9. Special assessments or taxation for local improvements. The legislature may vest the corporate authorities of cities, towns and villages with power to make local improvements by special assessment, or by special taxation of property benefited. For all corporate purposes, all municipal corporations may be vested with authority to assess and collect taxes and such taxes shall be uniform in respect to persons and property within the jurisdiction of the body levying the same.

Section 10. Retired persons property tax exemption. Notwithstanding the provisions of Article 7, section 1 (Amendment 14) and Article 7, section 2 (Amendment 17), the following tax exemption shall be allowed as to real property:

The legislature shall have the power, by appropriate legislation, to grant to retired property owners relief from the property tax on the real property occupied as a residence by those owners. The legislature may place such restrictions and conditions upon the granting of such relief as it shall deem proper. Such restrictions and conditions may include, but are not limited to, the limiting of the relief to those property owners below a specific level of income and those fulfilling certain minimum residential requirements. [Amendment 47, 1965 ex.s. House Joint Resolution No. 7, p 2821. Approved November 8, 1966.]

Section 11. Taxation based on actual use. Nothing in this Article VII as amended shall prevent the legislature from providing, subject to such conditions as it may enact, that the true and fair value in money (a) of farms, agricultural lands, standing timber and timberlands, and

(b) of other open space lands which are used for recreation or for enjoyment of their scenic or natural beauty shall be based on the use to which such property is currently applied, and such values shall be used in computing the assessed valuation of such property in the same manner as the assessed valuation is computed for all property. [Amendment 53, 1967 House Joint Resolution No. 1; see 1969 p 2976. Approved November 5, 1968.]

Section 12. Budget stabilization account. (a) A budget stabilization account shall be established and maintained in the state treasury.

(b) By June 30th of each fiscal year, an amount equal to one percent of the general state revenues for that fiscal year shall be transferred to the budget stabilization account. Nothing in this subsection (b) shall prevent the appropriation of additional amounts to the budget stabilization account.

(c) Each fiscal quarter, the state economic and revenue forecast council appointed and authorized as provided by statute, or successor entity, shall estimate state employment growth for the current and next two fiscal years.

(d) Moneys may be withdrawn and appropriated from the budget stabilization account as follows:

(i) If the governor declares a state of emergency resulting from a catastrophic event that necessitates government action to protect life or public safety, then for that fiscal year moneys may be withdrawn and appropriated from the budget stabilization account, via separate legislation setting forth the nature of the emergency and containing an appropriation limited to the above-authorized purposes as contained in the declaration, by a favorable vote of a majority of the members elected to each house of the legislature.

(ii) If the employment growth forecast for any fiscal year is estimated to be less than one percent, then for that fiscal year moneys may be withdrawn and appropriated from the budget stabilization account by the favorable vote of a majority of the members elected to each house of the legislature.

(iii) Any amount may be withdrawn and appropriated from the budget stabilization account at any time by the favorable vote of at least three-fifths of the members of each house of the legislature.

(e) Amounts in the budget stabilization account may be invested as provided by law and retained in that account. When the balance in the budget stabilization account, including investment earnings, equals more than ten percent of the estimated general state revenues in that fiscal year, the legislature by the favorable vote of a majority of the members elected to each house of the legislature may withdraw and appropriate the balance to the extent that the balance exceeds ten percent of the estimated general state revenues. Appropriations under this subsection (e) may be made solely for deposit to the education construction fund.

(f) As used in this section, "general state revenues" has the meaning set forth in Article VIII, section 1 of the Constitution. Forecasts and estimates shall be made by the state economic and revenue forecast council appointed and authorized as provided by statute, or successor entity.

(g) The legislature shall enact appropriate laws to carry out the purposes of this section.

(h) This section takes effect July 1, 2008. [Amendment 99, 2007 Engrossed Substitute Senate Joint Resolution No. 8206, pp 3146, 3147. Approved November 6, 2007.]

Article VIII
State, County, and Municipal Indebtedness

Section 1. State debt. (a) The state may contract debt, the principal of which shall be paid and discharged within thirty years from the time of contracting thereof, in the manner set forth herein.

(b) The aggregate debt contracted by the state shall not exceed that amount for which payments of principal and interest in any fiscal year would require the state to expend more than nine percent of the arithmetic mean of its general state revenues for the three immediately preceding fiscal years as certified by the treasurer. The term "fiscal year" means that period of time commencing July 1 of any year and ending on June 30 of the following year.

(c) The term "general state revenues" when used in this section, shall include all state money received in the treasury from each and every source whatsoever except: (1) Fees and revenues derived from the ownership or operation of any undertaking, facility, or project; (2) Moneys received as gifts, grants, donations, aid, or assistance or otherwise from the United States or any department, bureau, or corporation thereof, or any person, firm, or corporation, public or private, when the terms and conditions of such gift, grant, donation, aid, or assistance require the application and disbursement of such moneys otherwise than for the general purposes of the state of Washington; (3) Moneys to be paid into and received from retirement system funds, and performance bonds and deposits; (4) Moneys to be paid into and received from trust funds including but not limited to moneys received from taxes levied for specific purposes and the several permanent and irreducible funds of the state and the moneys derived therefrom but excluding bond redemption funds; (5) Proceeds received from the sale of bonds or other evidences of indebtedness.

(d) In computing the amount required for payment of principal and interest on outstanding debt under this section, debt shall be construed to mean borrowed money represented by bonds, notes, or other evidences of indebtedness which are secured by the full faith and credit of the state or are required to be repaid, directly or indirectly, from general state revenues and which are incurred by the state, any department, authority, public corporation, or quasi public corporation of the state, any state university or college, or any other public agency created by the state but not by counties, cities, towns, school districts, or other municipal corporations, but shall not include obligations for the payment of current expenses of state government, nor shall it include debt hereafter incurred pursuant to section 3 of this article, obligations guaranteed as provided for in subsection (g) of this section, principal of bond anticipation notes or obligations issued to fund or refund the indebtedness of the Washington state building authority. In addition, for the purpose of computing the amount required for payment of interest on outstanding debt under subsection (b) of this section and this subsection, "interest" shall be reduced by subtracting the amount scheduled to be received by the state as payments from the federal government in each year in respect of bonds, notes, or other evidences of indebtedness subject to this section.

(e) The state may pledge the full faith, credit, and taxing power of the state to guarantee the voter approved general obligation debt of school districts in the manner authorized by the legislature. Any such guarantee does not remove the debt obligation of the school district and is not state debt.

(f) The state may, without limitation, fund or refund, at or prior to maturity, the whole or any part of any existing debt or of any debt hereafter contracted pursuant to section 1, section 2, or section 3 of this article, including any premium payable with respect thereto and interest thereon, or fund or refund, at or prior to maturity, the whole or any part of any indebtedness incurred or authorized prior to the effective date of this amendment by any entity of the type described in subsection (h) of this section, including any premium payable with respect thereto and any interest thereon. Such funding or refunding shall not be deemed to be contracting debt by the state.

(g) Notwithstanding the limitation contained in subsection (b) of this section, the state may pledge its full faith, credit, and taxing power to guarantee the payment of any obligation payable from revenues received from any of the following sources: (1) Fees collected by the state as license fees for motor vehicles; (2) Excise taxes collected by the state on the sale, distribution or use of motor vehicle fuel; and (3) Interest on the permanent common school fund: Provided, That the legislature shall, at all times, provide sufficient revenues from such sources to pay the principal and interest due on all obligations for which said source of revenue is pledged.

(h) No money shall be paid from funds in custody

of the treasurer with respect to any debt contracted after the effective date of this amendment by the Washington state building authority, the capitol committee, or any similar entity existing or operating for similar purposes pursuant to which such entity undertakes to finance or provide a facility for use or occupancy by the state or any agency, department, or instrumentality thereof.

(i) The legislature shall prescribe all matters relating to the contracting, funding or refunding of debt pursuant to this section, including: The purposes for which debt may be contracted; by a favorable vote of three-fifths of the members elected to each house, the amount of debt which may be contracted for any class of such purposes; the kinds of notes, bonds, or other evidences of debt which may be issued by the state; and the manner by which the treasurer shall determine and advise the legislature, any appropriate agency, officer, or instrumentality of the state as to the available debt capacity within the limitation set forth in this section. The legislature may delegate to any state officer, agency, or instrumentality any of its powers relating to the contracting, funding or refunding of debt pursuant to this section except its power to determine the amount and purposes for which debt may be contracted.

(j) The full faith, credit, and taxing power of the state of Washington are pledged to the payment of the debt created on behalf of the state pursuant to this section and the legislature shall provide by appropriation for the payment of the interest upon and installments of principal of all such debt as the same falls due, but in any event, any court of record may compel such payment.

(k) Notwithstanding the limitations contained in subsection (b) of this section, the state may issue certificates of indebtedness in such sum or sums as may be necessary to meet temporary deficiencies of the treasury, to preserve the best interests of the state in the conduct of the various state institutions, departments, bureaus, and agencies during each fiscal year; such certificates may be issued only to provide for appropriations already made by the legislature and such certificates must be retired and the debt discharged other than by refunding within twelve months after the date of incurrence.

(l) Bonds, notes, or other obligations issued and sold by the state of Washington pursuant to and in conformity with this article shall not be invalid for any irregularity or defect in the proceedings of the issuance or sale thereof and shall be incontestable in the hands of a bona fide purchaser or holder thereof. [Amendment 103, 2010 Senate Joint Resolution No. 8225, p 3129-3132. Approved November 2, 2010.]

Section 2. Powers extended in certain cases. In addition to the above limited power to contract debts the state may contract debts to repel invasion, suppress insurrection, or to defend the state in war, but the money arising from the contracting of such debts shall be applied to the purpose for which it was raised and to no other purpose whatever.

Section 3. Special indebtedness, how authorized.
Except the debt specified in sections one and two of this article, no debts shall hereafter be contracted by, or on behalf of this state, unless such debt shall be authorized by law for some single work or object to be distinctly specified therein. No such law shall take effect until it shall, at a general election, or a special election called for that purpose, have been submitted to the people and have received a majority of all the votes cast for and against it at such election. [Amendment 60, part, 1971 House Joint Resolution No. 52, part, p 1836. Approved November, 1972.]

Section 4. Moneys disbursed only by appropriations.
No moneys shall ever be paid out of the treasury of this state, or any of its funds, or any of the funds under its management, except in pursuance of an appropriation by law; nor unless such payment be made within one calendar month after the end of the next ensuing fiscal biennium, and every such law making a new appropriation, or continuing or reviving an appropriation, shall distinctly specify the sum appropriated, and the object to which it is to be applied, and it shall not be sufficient for such law to refer to any other law to fix such sum. [Amendment 11, 1921 p 80 Section 1. Approved November, 1922.]

Section 5. Credit not to be loaned. The credit of the state shall not, in any manner be given or loaned to, or in aid of, any individual, association, company or corporation.

Section 6. Limitations upon municipal indebtedness.
No county, city, town, school district, or other municipal
corporation shall for any purpose become indebted in any
manner to an amount exceeding one and one-half per
centum of the taxable property in such county, city, town,
school district, or other municipal corporation, without
the assent of three-fifths of the voters therein voting
at an election to be held for that purpose, nor in cases
requiring such assent shall the total indebtedness at any
time exceed five per centum on the value of the taxable
property therein, to be ascertained by the last assessment
for state and county purposes previous to the incurring
of such indebtedness, except that in incorporated cities
the assessment shall be taken from the last assessment for
city purposes: *Provided,* That no part of the indebtedness
allowed in this section shall be incurred for any purpose
other than strictly county, city, town, school district, or
other municipal purposes: *Provided further,* That (a) any
city or town, with such assent, may be allowed to become
indebted to a larger amount, but not exceeding five per
centum additional for supplying such city or town with
water, artificial light, and sewers, when the works for
supplying such water, light, and sewers shall be owned and
controlled by the municipality and (b) any school district
with such assent, may be allowed to become indebted
to a larger amount but not exceeding five per centum
additional for capital outlays. [Amendment 27, 1951 House
Joint Resolution No. 8, p 961. Approved November 4,
1952.]

Section 7. Credit not to be loaned. No county, city, town or other municipal corporation shall hereafter give any money, or property, or loan its money, or credit to or in aid of any individual, association, company or corporation, except for the necessary support of the poor and infirm, or become directly or indirectly the owner of any stock in or bonds of any association, company or corporation.

Section 8. Port expenditures – Industrial development – Promotion. The use of public funds by port districts in such manner as may be prescribed by the legislature for industrial development or trade promotion and promotional hosting shall be deemed a public use for a public purpose, and shall not be deemed a gift within the provisions of section 7 of this Article. [Amendment 45, 1965 ex.s. Senate Joint Resolution No. 25, p 2819. Approved November 8, 1966.]

Section 9. State building authority. The legislature is empowered notwithstanding any other provision in this Constitution, to provide for a state building authority in corporate and politic form which may contract with agencies or departments of the state government to construct upon land owned by the state or its agencies, or to be acquired by the state building authority, buildings and appurtenant improvements which such state agencies or departments are hereby empowered to lease at reasonable rental rates from the Washington state building authority for terms up to seventy-five years with provisions for eventual vesting of title in the state or its agencies. This section shall not be construed as authority to provide buildings through lease or otherwise to nongovernmental entities. The legislature may authorize the state building authority to borrow funds solely upon its own credit and to issue bonds or other evidences of indebtedness therefor to be repaid from its revenues and to secure the same by pledging its income or mortgaging its leaseholds. The provisions of sections 1 and 3 of this article shall not apply to indebtedness incurred pursuant to this section. [Amendment 51, 1967 Senate Joint Resolution No. 17; see 1969 p 2976. Approved November 5, 1968.]

Section 10. Energy, water, or stormwater or sewer services conservation assistance. Notwithstanding the provisions of section 7 of this Article, any county, city, town, quasi municipal corporation, municipal corporation, or political subdivision of the state which is engaged in the sale or distribution of water, energy, or stormwater or sewer services may, as authorized by the legislature, use public moneys or credit derived from operating revenues from the sale of water, energy, or stormwater or sewer services to assist the owners of structures or equipment in financing the acquisition and installation of materials and equipment for the conservation or more efficient use of water, energy, or stormwater or sewer services in such structures or equipment. Except as provided in section 7 of this Article, an appropriate charge back shall be made for such extension of public moneys or credit and the same shall be a lien against the structure benefited or a security interest in the equipment benefited. Any financing for energy conservation authorized by this article shall only be used for conservation purposes in existing structures and shall not be used for any purpose which results in a conversion from one energy source to another. [Amendment 91, 1997 House Joint Resolution No. 4209, p 3065. Approved November 4, 1997.]

Section 11. Agricultural commodity assessments – Development, promotion, and hosting. The use of agricultural commodity assessments by agricultural commodity commissions in such manner as may be prescribed by the legislature for agricultural development or trade promotion and promotional hosting shall be deemed a public use for a public purpose, and shall not be deemed a gift within the provisions of section 5 of this article. [Amendment 76, 1985 House Joint Resolution No. 42, p 2402. Approved November 5, 1985.]

Article IX
Education

Section 1. Preamble. It is the paramount duty of the state to make ample provision for the education of all children residing within its borders, without distinction or preference on account of race, color, caste, or sex.

Section 2. Public school system. The legislature shall provide for a general and uniform system of public schools. The public school system shall include common schools, and such high schools, normal schools, and technical schools as may hereafter be established. But the entire revenue derived from the common school fund and the state tax for common schools shall be exclusively applied to the support of the common schools.

Section 3. Funds for support. The principal of the common school fund as the same existed on June 30, 1965, shall remain permanent and irreducible. The said fund shall consist of the principal amount thereof existing on June 30, 1965, and such additions thereto as may be derived after June 30, 1965, from the following named sources, to wit: Appropriations and donations by the state to this fund; donations and bequests by individuals to the state or public for common schools; the proceeds of lands and other property which revert to the state by escheat and forfeiture; the proceeds of all property granted to the state when the purpose of the grant is not specified, or is uncertain; funds accumulated in the treasury of the state for the disbursement of which provision has not been made by law; the proceeds of the sale of stone, minerals, or property other than timber and other crops from school and state lands, other than those granted for specific purposes; all moneys received from persons appropriating stone, minerals or property other than timber and other crops from school and state lands other than those granted for specific purposes, and all moneys other than rental recovered from persons trespassing on said lands; five per centum of the proceeds of the sale of public lands lying within the state, which shall be sold by the United States subsequent to the admission of the state into the Union as approved by section 13 of the act of congress enabling the admission of the state into the Union; the principal of all funds arising from the sale of lands and other property which have been, and hereafter may be granted to the state for the support of common schools. The legislature may make further provisions for enlarging said fund.

There is hereby established the common school construction fund to be used exclusively for the purpose of financing the construction of facilities for the common schools. The sources of said fund shall be: (1) Those proceeds derived from the sale or appropriation of timber and other crops from school and state lands subsequent to June 30, 1965, other than those granted for specific purposes; (2) the interest accruing on said permanent common school fund from and after July 1, 1967, together with all rentals and other revenues derived therefrom and from lands and other property devoted to the permanent common school fund from and after July 1, 1967; and (3) such other sources as the legislature may direct. That portion of the common school construction fund derived from interest on the permanent common school fund may be used to retire such bonds as may be authorized by law for the purpose of financing the construction of facilities for the common schools.

The interest accruing on the permanent common school fund together with all rentals and other revenues accruing thereto pursuant to subsection (2) of this section during the period after the effective date of this amendment and prior to July 1, 1967, shall be exclusively applied to the current use of the common schools.

To the extent that the moneys in the common school construction fund are in excess of the amount necessary to allow fulfillment of the purpose of said fund, the excess shall be available for deposit to the credit of the permanent common school fund or available for the current use of the common schools, as the legislature may direct. [Amendment 43, 1965 ex.s. Senate Joint Resolution No. 22, part 1, p 2817. Approved November 8, 1966.]

Section 4. Sectarian control or influence prohibited. All schools maintained or supported wholly or in part by the public funds shall be forever free from sectarian control or influence.

Section 5. Loss of permanent fund to become state debt. All losses to the permanent common school or any other state educational fund, which shall be occasioned by defalcation, mismanagement or fraud of the agents or officers controlling or managing the same, shall be audited by the proper authorities of the state. The amount so audited shall be a permanent funded debt against the state in favor of the particular fund sustaining such loss, upon which not less than six per cent annual interest shall be paid. The amount of liability so created shall not be counted as a part of the indebtedness authorized and limited elsewhere in this Constitution.

Article X
Militia

Section 1. Who liable to military duty. All able-bodied male citizens of this state between the ages of eighteen (18) and forty-five (45) years except such as are exempt by laws of the United States or by the laws of this state, shall be liable to military duty.

Section 2. Organization – Discipline – Officers – Power to call out. The legislature shall provide by law for organizing and disciplining the militia in such manner as it may deem expedient, not incompatible with the Constitution and laws of the United States. Officers of the militia shall be elected or appointed in such manner as the legislature shall from time to time direct and shall be commissioned by the governor. The governor shall have power to call forth the militia to execute the laws of the state to suppress insurrections and repel invasions.

Section 3. Soldiers' home. The legislature shall provide by law for the maintenance of a soldiers' home for honorably discharged Union soldiers, sailors, marines and members of the state militia disabled while in the line of duty and who are *bona fide* citizens of the state.

Section 4. Public arms. The legislature shall provide by law, for the protection and safe keeping of the public arms.

Section 5. Privilege from arrest. The militia shall, in all cases, except treason, felony and breach of the peace, be privileged from arrest during their attendance at musters and elections of officers, and in going to and returning from the same.

Section 6. Exemption from military duty. No person or persons, having conscientious scruples against bearing arms, shall be compelled to do militia duty in time of peace: *Provided,* such person or persons shall pay an equivalent for such exemption.

Article XI
County, City, and Township Organization

Section 1. Existing counties recognized. The several counties of the Territory of Washington existing at the time of the adoption of this Constitution are hereby recognized as legal subdivisions of this state.

Section 2. County seats – Location and removal. No county seat shall be removed unless three-fifths of the qualified electors of the county, voting on the proposition at a general election shall vote in favor of such removal, and three-fifths of all votes cast on the proposition shall be required to relocate a county seat. A proposition of removal shall not be submitted in the same county more than once in four years.

Section 3. New counties. No new counties shall be established which shall reduce any county to a population less than four thousand (4,000), nor shall a new county be formed containing a less population than two thousand (2,000). There shall be no territory stricken from any county unless a majority of the voters living in such territory shall petition therefor and then only under such other conditions as may be prescribed by a general law applicable to the whole state. Every county which shall be enlarged or created from territory taken from any other county or counties shall be liable for a just proportion of the existing debts and liabilities of the county or counties from which such territory shall be taken: *Provided,* That in such accounting neither county shall be charged with any debt or liability then existing incurred in the purchase of any county property, or in the purchase or construction of any county buildings then in use, or under construction, which shall fall within and be retained by the county: *Provided further,* That this shall not be construed to affect the rights of creditors.

Section 4. County government and township organization. The legislature shall establish a system of county government, which shall be uniform throughout the state except as hereinafter provided, and by general laws shall provide for township organization, under which any county may organize whenever a majority of the qualified electors of such county voting at a general election shall so determine; and whenever a county shall adopt township organization, the assessment and collection of the revenue shall be made, and the business of such county and the local affairs of the several townships therein, shall be managed and transacted in the manner prescribed by such general law.

Any county may frame a "Home Rule" charter for its own government subject to the Constitution and laws of this state, and for such purpose the legislative authority of such county may cause an election to be had, at which election there shall be chosen by the qualified voters of said county not less than fifteen (15) nor more than twenty-five (25) freeholders thereof, as determined by the legislative authority, who shall have been residents of said county for a period of at least five (5) years preceding their election and who are themselves qualified electors, whose duty it shall be to convene within thirty (30) days after their election and prepare and propose a charter for such county. Such proposed charter shall be submitted to the qualified electors of said county, and if a majority of such qualified electors voting thereon ratify the same, it shall become the charter of said county and shall become the organic law thereof, and supersede any existing charter, including amendments thereto, or any existing form of county government, and all special laws inconsistent with such charter. Said proposed charter shall be published in two (2) legal newspapers published in said county, at least once a week for four (4) consecutive weeks prior to the day of submitting the same to the electors for their approval as above provided. All elections in this section authorized shall only be had upon notice, which notice shall specify the object of calling such election and shall be given for at least ten (10) days before the day of election in all election districts of said county. Said elections may be general or special elections and except as herein provided, shall be governed by the law regulating and controlling general or special elections in said county. Such charter may be amended by proposals therefor submitted by the legislative authority of said county to the electors thereof at any general election after notice of such submission published as above specified, and ratified by a majority of the qualified electors voting thereon. In submitting any such charter or amendment thereto, any alternate article or proposition may be presented for the choice of the voters and may be voted on separately without prejudice to others.

Any home rule charter proposed as herein provided, may provide for such county officers as may be deemed necessary to carry out and perform all county functions as provided by charter or by general law, and for their compensation, but shall not affect the election of the prosecuting attorney, the county superintendent of schools, the judges of the superior court, and the justices of the peace, or the jurisdiction of the courts.

Notwithstanding the foregoing provision for the calling of an election by the legislative authority of such county for the election of freeholders to frame a county charter, registered voters equal in number to ten (10) per centum of the voters of any such county voting at the last preceding general election, may at any time propose by petition the calling of an election of freeholders. The petition shall be filed with the county auditor of the county at least three (3) months before any general election and the proposal that a board of freeholders be elected for the purpose of framing a county charter shall be submitted to the vote of the people at said general election, and at the same election a board of freeholders of not less than fifteen (15) or more than twenty-five (25), as fixed in the petition calling for the election, shall be chosen to draft the new charter. The procedure for the nomination of qualified electors as candidates for said board of freeholders shall be prescribed by the legislative authority of the county, and the procedure for the framing of the charter and the submission of the charter as framed shall be the same as in the case of a board of freeholders chosen at an election initiated by the legislative authority of the county.

In calling for any election of freeholders as provided in this section, the legislative authority of the county shall apportion the number of freeholders to be elected in accordance with either the legislative districts or the county commissioner districts, if any, within said county, the number of said freeholders to be elected from each of said districts to be in proportion to the population of said districts as nearly as may be.

Should the charter proposed receive the affirmative vote of the majority of the electors voting thereon, the legislative authority of the county shall immediately call such special election as may be provided for therein, if any, and the county government shall be established in accordance with the terms of said charter not more than six (6) months after the election at which the charter was adopted.

The terms of all elective officers, except the prosecuting attorney, the county superintendent of schools, the judges of the superior court, and the justices of the peace, who are in office at the time of the adoption of a Home Rule Charter shall terminate as provided in the charter. All appointive officers in office at the time the charter goes into effect, whose positions are not abolished thereby, shall continue until their successors shall have qualified.

After the adoption of such charter, such county shall continue to have all the rights, powers, privileges and benefits then possessed or thereafter conferred by general law. All the powers, authority and duties granted to and imposed on county officers by general law, except the prosecuting attorney, the county superintendent of schools, the judges of the superior court and the justices of the peace, shall be vested in the legislative authority of the county unless expressly vested in specific officers by the charter. The legislative authority may by resolution delegate any of its executive or administrative powers, authority or duties not expressly vested in specific officers by the charter, to any county officer or officers or county employee or employees.

The provisions of sections 5, 6, 7, and the first sentence of section 8 of this Article as amended shall not apply to counties in which the government has been established by charter adopted under the provisions hereof. The authority conferred on the board of county commissioners by Section 15 of Article II as amended, shall be exercised by the legislative authority of the county. [Amendment 21, 1947 Senate Joint Resolution No. 5, p 1372. Approved November 2, 1948.]

Section 5. County government. The legislature, by general and uniform laws, shall provide for the election in the several counties of boards of county commissioners, sheriffs, county clerks, treasurers, prosecuting attorneys and other county, township or precinct and district officers, as public convenience may require, and shall prescribe their duties, and fix their terms of office: *Provided,* That the legislature may, by general laws, classify the counties by population and provide for the election in certain classes of counties certain officers who shall exercise the powers and perform the duties of two or more officers. It shall regulate the compensation of all such officers, in proportion to their duties, and for that purpose may classify the counties by population: *Provided,* That it may delegate to the legislative authority of the counties the right to prescribe the salaries of its own members and the salaries of other county officers. And it shall provide for the strict accountability of such officers for all fees which may be collected by them and for all public moneys which may be paid to them, or officially come into their possession. [Amendment 57, part, 1971 Senate Joint Resolution No. 38, part, p 1829. Approved November, 1972.]

Section 6. Vacancies in township, precinct or road district office. The board of county commissioners in each county shall fill all vacancies occurring in any township, precinct or road district office of such county by appointment, and officers thus appointed shall hold office till the next general election, and until their successors are elected and qualified. [Amendment 52, part, 1967 Senate Joint Resolution No. 24, part. Approved November 5, 1968.]

Section 7. Tenure of office limited to two terms.
[Repealed by Amendment 22, 1947 House Joint Resolution
No. 4, p 1385. Approved November 2, 1948.]

Section 8. Salaries and limitations affecting. The
salary of any county, city, town, or municipal officers shall
not be increased except as provided in section 1 of Article
XXX or diminished after his election, or during his term
of office; nor shall the term of any such officer be extended
beyond the period for which he is elected or appointed.
[Amendment 57, art, 1971 Senate Joint Resolution No. 38,
part, p 1829. Approved November, 1972.]

Section 9. State taxes not to be released or commuted.
No county, nor the inhabitants thereof, nor the property
therein, shall be released or discharged from its or their
proportionate share of taxes to be levied for state purposes,
nor shall commutation for such taxes be authorized in any
form whatever.

Section 10. Incorporation of municipalities.
Corporations for municipal purposes shall not be created
by special laws; but the legislature, by general laws,
shall provide for the incorporation, organization and
classification in proportion to population, of cities and
towns, which laws may be altered, amended or repealed.
Cities and towns heretofore organized, or incorporated
may become organized under such general laws whenever
a majority of the electors voting at a general election, shall

so determine, and shall organize in conformity therewith; and cities or towns heretofore or hereafter organized, and all charters thereof framed or adopted by authority of this Constitution shall be subject to and controlled by general laws. Any city containing a population of ten thousand inhabitants, or more, shall be permitted to frame a charter for its own government, consistent with and subject to the Constitution and laws of this state, and for such purpose the legislative authority of such city may cause an election to be had at which election there shall be chosen by the qualified electors of said city, fifteen freeholders thereof, who shall have been residents of said city for a period of at least two years preceding their election and qualified electors, whose duty it shall be to convene within ten days after their election, and prepare and propose a charter for such city. Such proposed charter shall be submitted to the qualified electors of said city, and if a majority of such qualified electors voting thereon ratify the same, it shall become the charter of said city, and shall become the organic law thereof, and supersede any existing charter including amendments thereto, and all special laws inconsistent with such charter. Said proposed charter shall be published in the daily newspaper of largest general circulation published in the area to be incorporated as a first class city under the charter or, if no daily newspaper is published therein, then in the newspaper having the largest general circulation within such area at least once each week for four weeks next preceding the day of submitting the same to the electors for their approval, as above provided. All elections in this section authorized shall only be had upon notice, which notice shall specify the object of calling such election, and shall be given as required by law. Said elections may be general or special elections, and except as herein provided shall be governed by the law regulating and controlling general or special elections in said city. Such charter may be amended by proposals therefor submitted by the legislative authority of such city to the electors thereof at any general election after notice of said submission published as above specified, and ratified by a majority of the qualified electors voting thereon. In submitting any such charter, or amendment thereto, any alternate article or proposition may be presented for the choice of the voters, and may be voted on separately without prejudice to others. [Amendment 40, 1963 ex.s. Senate Joint Resolution No. 1, p 1526. Approved November 3, 1964.]

Section 11. Police and sanitary regulations. Any county, city, town or township may make and enforce within its limits all such local police, sanitary and other regulations as are not in conflict with general laws.

Section 12. Assessment and collection of taxes in municipalities. The legislature shall have no power to impose taxes upon counties, cities, towns or other municipal corporations, or upon the inhabitants or property thereof, for county, city, town, or other municipal purposes, but may, by general laws, vest in the corporate authorities thereof, the power to assess and collect taxes for such purposes.

Section 13. Private property, when may be taken for public debt. Private property shall not be taken or sold for the payment of the corporate debt of any public or municipal corporation, except in the mode provided by law for the levy and collection of taxes.

Section 14. Private use of public funds prohibited. The making of profit out of county, city, town, or other public money, or using the same for any purpose not authorized by law, by any officer having the possession or control thereof, shall be a felony, and shall be prosecuted and punished as prescribed by law.

Section 15. Deposit of public funds. All moneys, assessments and taxes belonging to or collected for the use of any county, city, town or other public or municipal corporation, coming into the hands of any officer thereof, shall immediately be deposited with the treasurer, or other legal depositary to the credit of such city, town, or other corporation respectively, for the benefit of the funds to which they belong.

Section 16. Combined city-county. Any county may frame a "Home Rule" charter subject to the Constitution and laws of this state to provide for the formation and government of combined city and county municipal corporations, each of which shall be known as "city-county". Registered voters equal in number to ten (10) percent of the voters of any such county voting at the last preceding general election may at any time propose by a petition the calling of an election of freeholders. The provisions of section 4 of this Article with respect to a petition calling for an election of freeholders to frame a county home rule charter, the election of freeholders, and the framing and adoption of a county home rule charter pursuant to such petition shall apply to a petition proposed under this section for the election of freeholders to frame a city-county charter, the election of freeholders, and to the framing and adoption of such city-county charter pursuant to such petition. Except as otherwise provided in this section, the provisions of section 4 applicable to a county home rule charter shall apply to a city-county charter. If there are not sufficient legal newspapers published in the county to meet the requirements for publication of a proposed charter under section 4 of this Article, publication in a legal newspaper circulated in the county may be substituted for publication in a legal newspaper published in the county. No such "city-county" shall be formed except by a majority vote of the qualified electors voting thereon in the county. The charter shall designate the respective officers of such city-county who shall perform the duties imposed by law upon county officers. Every such city-county shall have and enjoy all rights, powers and privileges asserted in its charter, and in addition thereto, such rights, powers and privileges as may be granted to it, or to any city or county or class or classes of cities and counties. In the event of a conflict in the constitutional provisions applying to cities and those applying to counties or of a conflict in the general laws applying to cities and those applying to counties, a city-county shall be authorized to exercise any powers that are granted to either the cities or the counties.

No legislative enactment which is a prohibition or restriction shall apply to the rights, powers and privileges of a city-county unless such prohibition or restriction shall apply equally to every other city, county, and city-county.

The provisions of sections 2, 3, 5, 6, and 8 and of the first paragraph of section 4 of this article shall not apply to any such city-county.

Municipal corporations may be retained or otherwise provided for within the city-county. The formation, powers and duties of such municipal corporations shall be prescribed by the charter.

No city-county shall for any purpose become indebted in any manner to an amount exceeding three per centum of the taxable property in such city-county without the assent of three-fifths of the voters therein voting at an election to be held for that purpose, nor in cases requiring such assent shall the total indebtedness at any time exceed ten per centum of the value of the taxable property therein, to be ascertained by the last assessment for city-county purposes previous to the incurring of such indebtedness: *Provided,* That no part of the indebtedness allowed in this section shall be incurred for any purpose other than strictly city-county or other municipal purposes: *Provided further,* That any city-county, with such assent may be allowed to become indebted to a larger amount, but not exceeding five per centum additional for supplying such city-county with water, artificial light, and sewers, when the works for supplying such water, light, and sewers shall be owned and controlled by the city-county.

No municipal corporation which is retained or otherwise provided for within the city-county shall for any purpose become indebted in any manner to an amount exceeding one and one-half per centum of the taxable property in such municipal corporation without the assent of three-fifths of the voters therein voting at an election to be held for that purpose, nor shall the total indebtedness at any time exceed five per centum of the value of the taxable property therein, to be ascertained by the last assessment for city-county purposes previous to the incurring of such indebtedness: *Provided,* That no part of the indebtedness allowed in this section shall be incurred for any purpose other than strictly municipal purposes: *Provided further,* That any such municipal corporation, with such assent, may be allowed to become indebted to a larger amount, but not exceeding five per centum additional for supplying such municipal corporation with water, artificial light, and sewers, when the works for supplying such water, light, and sewers shall be owned and controlled by the municipal corporation. All taxes which are levied and collected within a municipal corporation for a specific purpose shall be expended within that municipal corporation.

The authority conferred on the city-county government shall not be restricted by the second sentence of Article 7, section 1, or by Article 8, section 6 of this Constitution. [Amendment 58, 1971 House Joint Resolution No. 21, p 1831. Approved November, 1972.]

Article XII
Corporations Other Than Municipal

Section 1. Corporations, how formed. Corporations may be formed under general laws, but shall not be created by special acts. All laws relating to corporations may be altered, amended or repealed by the legislature at any time, and all corporations doing business in this state may, as to such business, be regulated, limited or restrained by law.

Section 2. Existing charters. All existing charters, franchises, special or exclusive privileges, under which an actual and *bona fide* organization shall not have taken place, and business been commenced in good faith, at the time of the adoption of this Constitution shall thereafter have no validity.

Section 3. Existing charters not to be extended nor forfeiture remitted. The legislature shall not extend any franchise or charter, nor remit the forfeiture of any franchise or charter of any corporation now existing, or which shall hereafter exist under the laws of this state.

Section 4. Liability of stockholders. Each stockholder in all incorporated companies, except corporations organized for banking or insurance purposes, shall be liable for the debts of the corporation to the amount of his unpaid stock and no more; and one or more stockholders may be joined as parties defendant in suits to recover upon this liability.

Section 5. Term "corporation," defined – Right to sue and be sued. The term corporations, as used in this article, shall be construed to include all associations and joint stock companies having any powers or privileges of corporations not possessed by individuals or partnerships, and all corporations shall have the right to sue and shall be subject to be sued, in all courts, in like cases as natural persons.

Section 6. Limitations upon issuance of stock. Corporations shall not issue stock, except to *bona fide* subscribers therefor, or their assignees; nor shall any corporation issue any bond, or other obligation, for the payment of money, except for money or property received or labor done. The stock of corporations shall not be increased, except in pursuance of a general law, nor shall any law authorize the increase of stock, without the consent of the person or persons holding the larger amount in value of the stock, nor without due notice of the proposed increase having been previously given in such manner as may be prescribed by law. All fictitious increase of stock or indebtedness shall be void.

Section 7. Foreign corporations. No corporation organized outside the limits of this state shall be allowed to transact business within the state on more favorable conditions than are prescribed by law to similar corporations organized under the laws of this state.

Section 8. Alienation of franchise not to release liabilities. No corporation shall lease or alienate any franchise, so as to relieve the franchise, or property held thereunder, from the liabilities of the lessor, or grantor, lessee, or grantee, contracted or incurred in the operation, use, or enjoyment of such franchise or any of its privileges.

Section 9. State not to loan its credit or subscribe for stock. The state shall not in any manner loan its credit, nor shall it subscribe to, or be interested in the stock of any company, association or corporation.

Section 10. Eminent domain affecting. The exercise of the right of eminent domain shall never be so abridged or construed as to prevent the legislature from taking the property and franchises of incorporated companies, and subjecting them to public use the same as the property of individuals.

Section 11. Stockholder liability. No corporation, association, or individual shall issue or put in circulation as money anything but the lawful money of the United States. Each stockholder of any banking or insurance corporation or joint stock association shall be individually and personally liable equally and ratably, and not one for another, for all contracts, debts, and engagements of such corporation or association accruing while they remain such stockholders, to the extent of the amount of their stock therein at the par value thereof, in addition to the amount invested in such shares.

The legislature may provide that stockholders of banking corporations organized under the laws of this state which shall provide and furnish, either through membership in the Federal Deposit Insurance Corporation, or through membership in any other instrumentality of the government of the United States, insurance or security for the payment of the debts and obligations of such banking corporation equivalent to that required by the laws of the United States to be furnished and provided by national banking associations, shall be relieved from liability for the debts and obligations of such banking corporation to the same extent that stockholders of national banking associations are relieved from liability for the debts and obligations of such national banking associations under the laws of the United States. [Amendment 16, 1939 Senate Joint Resolution No. 8, p 1024. Approved November, 1940.]

Section 12. Receiving deposits by bank after insolvency. Any president, director, manager, cashier, or other officer of any banking institution, who shall receive or assent to the reception of deposits, after he shall have knowledge of the fact that such banking institution is insolvent or in failing circumstances, shall be individually responsible for such deposits so received.

Section 13. Common carriers, regulation of. All railroad, canal and other transportation companies are declared to be common carriers and subject to legislative control. Any association or corporation organized for the purpose, under the laws of this state, shall have the right to connect at the state line with railroads of other states. Every railroad company shall have the right with its road, whether the same be now constructed or may hereafter be constructed, to intersect, cross or connect with any other railroad, and when such railroads are of the same or similar gauge they shall at all crossings and at all points, where a railroad shall begin or terminate at or near any other railroad, form proper connections so that the cars of any such railroad companies may be speedily transferred from one railroad to another. All railroad companies shall receive and transport each the other's passengers, tonnage and cars without delay or discrimination.

Section 14. Prohibition against combinations by carriers. [Repealed by Amendment 67, 1977 House Joint Resolution No. 57, p 1714. Approved November 8, 1977.]

Section 15. Prohibition against discriminating charges. No discrimination in charges or facilities for transportation shall be made by any railroad or other transportation company between places or persons, or in the facilities for the transportation of the same classes of freight or passengers within this state, or coming from or going to any other state. Persons and property transported over any railroad, or by any other transportation company, or individual, shall be delivered at any station, landing or port, at charges not exceeding the charges for the transportation of persons and property of the same class, in the same direction, to any more distant station, port or landing. Excursion and commutation tickets may be issued at special rates.

Section 16. Prohibition against consolidating of competing lines. No railroad corporation shall consolidate its stock, property or franchises with any other railroad corporation owning a competing line.

Section 17. Rolling stock, personalty for purpose of taxation. The rolling stock and other movable property belonging to any railroad company or corporation in this state, shall be considered personal property, and shall be liable to taxation and to execution and sale in the same manner as the personal property of individuals and such property shall not be exempted from execution and sale.

Section 18. Rates for transportation. The legislature may pass laws establishing reasonable rates of charges for the transportation of passengers and freight, and to correct abuses and prevent discrimination and extortion in the rates of freight and passenger tariffs on the different railroads and other common carriers in the state, and shall enforce such laws by adequate penalties. A railroad and transportation commission may be established and its powers and duties fully defined by law. [Amendment 66, 1977 House Joint Resolution No. 55, p 1713. Approved November 8, 1977.]

Section 19. Telegraph and telephone companies. Any association or corporation, or the lessees or managers thereof, organized for the purpose, or any individual, shall have the right to construct and maintain lines of telegraph and telephone within this state, and said companies shall receive and transmit each other's messages without delay or discrimination and all of such companies are hereby declared to be common carriers and subject to legislative control. Railroad corporations organized or doing business in this state shall allow telegraph and telephone corporations and companies to construct and maintain telegraph lines on and along the rights of way of such railroads and railroad companies, and no railroad corporation organized or doing business in this state shall allow any telegraph corporation or company any facilities, privileges or rates for transportation of men or material or for repairing their lines not allowed to all telegraph companies. The right of eminent domain is hereby extended to all telegraph and telephone companies. The legislature shall, by general law of uniform operation, provide reasonable regulations to give effect to this section.

Section 20. Prohibition against free transportation for public officers. No railroad or other transportation company shall grant free passes, or sell tickets or passes at a discount, other than as sold to the public generally, to any member of the legislature, or to any person holding any public office within this state. The legislature shall pass laws to carry this provision into effect.

Section 21. Express companies. Railroad companies now or hereafter organized or doing business in this state, shall allow all express companies organized or doing business in this state, transportation over all lines of railroad owned or operated by such railroad companies upon equal terms with any other express company, and no railroad corporation organized or doing business in this state shall allow any express corporation or company any facilities, privileges or rates for transportation of men or materials or property carried by them or for doing the business of such express companies not allowed to all express companies.

Section 22. Monopolies and trusts. Monopolies and trusts shall never be allowed in this state, and no incorporated company, copartnership, or association of persons in this state shall directly or indirectly combine or make any contract with any other incorporated company, foreign or domestic, through their stockholders, or the trustees or assignees of such stockholders, or with any copartnership or association of persons, or in any manner whatever for the purpose of fixing the price or limiting the production or regulating the transportation of any product or commodity. The legislature shall pass laws for the enforcement of this section by adequate penalties, and in case of incorporated companies, if necessary for that purpose, may declare a forfeiture of their franchises.

Article XIII
State Institutions

Section 1. Educational, reformatory, and penal institutions. Educational, reformatory, and penal institutions; those for the benefit of youth who are blind or deaf or otherwise disabled; for persons who are mentally ill or developmentally disabled; and such other institutions as the public good may require, shall be fostered and supported by the state, subject to such regulations as may be provided by law. The regents, trustees, or commissioners of all such institutions existing at the time of the adoption of this Constitution, and of such as shall thereafter be established by law, shall be appointed by the governor, by and with the advice and consent of the senate; and upon all nominations made by the governor, the question shall be taken by ayes and noes, and entered upon the journal. [Amendment 83, 1988 House Joint Resolution No. 4231, p 1553. Approved November 8, 1988.]

Article XIV
Seat of Government

Section 1. State capital, location of. The legislature shall have no power to change, or to locate the seat of government of this state; but the question of the permanent location of the seat of government of the state shall be submitted to the qualified electors of the Territory, at the election to be held for the adoption of this Constitution. A majority of all the votes cast at said election, upon said question, shall be necessary to determine the permanent location of the seat of government for the state; and no place shall ever be the seat of government which shall not receive a majority of the votes cast on that matter. In case there shall be no choice of location at said first election the legislature shall, at its first regular session after the adoption of this Constitution, provide for submitting to the qualified electors of the state, at the next succeeding general election thereafter, the question of choice of location between the three places for which the highest number of votes shall have been cast at the said first election. Said legislature shall provide further that in case there shall be no choice of location at said second election, the question of choice between the two places for which the highest number of votes shall have been cast, shall be submitted in like manner to the qualified electors of the state at the next ensuing general election: *Provided,* That until the seat of government shall have been permanently located as herein provided, the temporary location thereof shall remain at the city of Olympia.

Section 2. Change of state capital. When the seat of government shall have been located as herein provided, the location thereof shall not thereafter be changed except by a vote of two-thirds of all the qualified electors of the state voting on that question, at a general election, at which the question of location of the seat of government shall have been submitted by the legislature.

Section 3. Restrictions on appropriations for capitol buildings. The legislature shall make no appropriations or expenditures for capitol buildings or grounds, except to keep the Territorial capitol buildings and grounds in repair, and for making all necessary additions thereto, until the seat of government shall have been permanently located, and the public buildings are erected at the permanent capital in pursuance of law.

Article XV
Harbors and Tide Waters

Section 1. Harbor line commission and restraint on disposition. The legislature shall provide for the appointment of a commission whose duty it shall be to locate and establish harbor lines in the navigable waters of all harbors, estuaries, bays and inlets of this state, wherever such navigable waters lie within or in front of the corporate limits of any city, or within one mile thereof on either side. Any harbor line so located or established may thereafter be changed, relocated or reestablished by the commission pursuant to such provision as may be made therefor by the legislature. The state shall never give, sell or lease to any private person, corporation, or association any rights whatever in the waters beyond such harbor lines, nor shall any of the area lying between any harbor line and the line of ordinary high water, and within not less than fifty feet nor more than two thousand feet of such harbor line (as the commission shall determine) be sold or granted by the state, nor its rights to control the same relinquished, but such area shall be forever reserved for landings, wharves, streets, and other conveniences of navigation and commerce. [Amendment 15, 1931 p 417 Section 1. Approved November, 1932.]

Section 2. Leasing and maintenance of wharves, docks, etc. The legislature shall provide general laws for the leasing of the right to build and maintain wharves, docks and other structures, upon the areas mentioned in section one of this article, but no lease shall be made for any term longer than thirty years, or the legislature may provide by general laws for the building and maintaining upon such area wharves, docks, and other structures.

Section 3. Extension of streets over tide lands. Municipal corporations shall have the right to extend their streets over intervening tide lands to and across the area reserved as herein provided.

Article XVI
School and Granted Lands

Section 1. Disposition of. All the public lands granted to the state are held in trust for all the people and none of such lands, nor any estate or interest therein, shall ever be disposed of unless the full market value of the estate or interest disposed of, to be ascertained in such manner as may be provided by law, be paid or safely secured to the state; nor shall any lands which the state holds by grant from the United States (in any case in which the manner of disposal and minimum price are so prescribed) be disposed of except in the manner and for at least the price prescribed in the grant thereof, without the consent of the United States.

Section 2. Manner and terms of sale. None of the lands granted to the state for educational purposes shall be sold otherwise than at public auction to the highest bidder, the value thereof, less the improvements shall, before any sale, be appraised by a board of appraisers to be provided by law, the terms of payment also to be prescribed by law, and no sale shall be valid unless the sum bid be equal to the appraised value of said land. In estimating the value of such lands for disposal, the value of the improvements thereon shall be excluded: *Provided,* That the sale of all school and university land heretofore made by the commissioners of any county or the university commissioners when the purchase price has been paid in good faith, may be confirmed by the legislature.

Section 3. Limitations on sales.

No more than one-fourth of the land granted to the state for educational purposes shall be sold prior to January 1, 1895, and not more than one-half prior to January 1, 1905: *provided,* that nothing herein shall be so construed as to prevent the state from selling the timber or stone off of any of the state lands in such manner and on such terms as may be prescribed by law: and *provided, further,* that no sale of timber lands shall be valid unless the full value of such lands is paid or secured to the state.

Section 4. How much may be offered in certain cases – Platting of.

No more than one hundred and sixty (160) acres of any granted lands of the state shall be offered for sale in one parcel, and all lands within the limits of any incorporated city or within two miles of the boundary of any incorporated city where the valuation of such land shall be found by appraisement to exceed one hundred dollars ($100) per acre shall, before the same be sold, be platted into lots and blocks of not more than five acres in a block, and not more than one block shall be offered for sale in one parcel.

Section 5. Investment of permanent common school fund.

The permanent common school fund of this state may be invested as authorized by law. [Amendment 44,

1965 ex.s. Senate Joint Resolution No. 22, part 2, p 2817.
Approved November 8, 1966.]

Section 6. Investment of higher education permanent funds. Notwithstanding the provisions of Article VIII, sections 5 and 7 and Article XII, section 9, or any other section or article of the Constitution of the state of Washington, the moneys of the permanent funds established for any of the institutions of higher education in this state may be invested as authorized by law. Without limitation, this shall include the authority to invest permanent funds held for the benefit of institutions of higher education in stocks or bonds issued by any association, company, or corporation if authorized by law. [Amendment 102, 2007 Substitute House Joint Resolution No. 4215, p 3145. Approved November 6, 2007.]

Article XVII
Tide Lands

Section 1. Declaration of state ownership. The state of Washington asserts its ownership to the beds and shores of all navigable waters in the state up to and including the line of ordinary high tide, in waters where the tide ebbs and flows, and up to and including the line of ordinary high water within the banks of all navigable rivers and lakes: *Provided,* that this section shall not be construed so as to debar any person from asserting his claim to vested rights in the courts of the state.

Section 2. Disclaimer of certain lands. The state of Washington disclaims all title in and claim to all tide, swamp and overflowed lands, patented by the United States: *Provided,* the same is not impeached for fraud.

Article XVIII
State Seal

Section 1. Seal of the state. The seal of the State of Washington shall be, a seal encircled with the words: "The Seal of the State of Washington," with the vignette of General George Washington as the central figure, and beneath the vignette the figures "1889."

Article XIX
Exemptions

Section 1. Exemptions - homesteads, etc. The legislature shall protect by law from forced sale a certain portion of the homestead and other property of all heads of families.

Article XX
Public Health and Vital Statistics

Section 1. Board of health and bureau of vital statistics. There shall be established by law a state board of health and a bureau of vital statistics in connection therewith, with such powers as the legislature may direct.

Section 2. Regulations concerning medicine, surgery and pharmacy. The legislature shall enact laws to regulate the practice of medicine and surgery, and the sale of drugs and medicines.

Article XXI
Water and Water Rights

Section 1. Public use of water. The use of the waters of this state for irrigation, mining and manufacturing purposes shall be deemed a public use.

Article XXII
Legislative Apportionment

Section 1. Senatorial apportionment. Until otherwise provided by law, the state shall be divided into twenty-four (24) senatorial districts, and said districts shall be constituted and numbered as follows: The counties of Stevens and Spokane shall constitute the first district, and be entitled to one senator; the county of Spokane shall constitute the second district, and be entitled to three senators; the county of Lincoln shall constitute the third district, and be entitled to one senator; the counties of Okanogan, Lincoln, Adams and Franklin shall constitute the fourth district, and be entitled to one senator; the county of Whitman shall constitute the fifth district, and be entitled to three senators; the counties of Garfield and Asotin shall constitute the sixth district, and be entitled to one senator; the county of Columbia shall constitute the seventh district, and be entitled to one senator; the county of Walla Walla shall constitute the eighth district, and be entitled to two senators; the counties of Yakima and Douglas shall constitute the ninth district, and be entitled to one senator; the county of Kittitas shall constitute the tenth district and be entitled to one senator; the counties of Klickitat, and Skamania shall constitute the eleventh district, and be entitled to one senator; the county of Clarke shall constitute the twelfth district, and be entitled to one senator; the county of Cowlitz shall constitute the thirteenth district, and be entitled to one senator; the county of Lewis shall constitute the fourteenth district, and be entitled to one senator; the counties of Pacific and Wahkiakum shall constitute the fifteenth district, and be entitled to one senator; the county of Thurston shall constitute the sixteenth district, and be entitled to one senator; the county of Chehalis shall constitute the seventeenth district, and be entitled to one senator; the county of Pierce shall constitute the eighteenth district, and be entitled to three senators; the county of King shall constitute the nineteenth district, and be entitled to five senators; the counties of Mason and Kitsap shall constitute the twentieth district, and be entitled to one senator; the counties of Jefferson, Clallam and San Juan shall constitute the twenty-first district, and be entitled to one senator; the county of Snohomish shall constitute the twenty-second district, and shall be entitled to one senator; the counties of Skagit and Island shall constitute the twenty-third district, and be entitled to one senator;

the county of Whatcom shall constitute the twenty-fourth district, and be entitled to one senator.

Section 2. Apportionment of representatives. Until otherwise provided by law the representatives shall be divided among the several counties of the state in the following manner; the county of Adams shall have one representative; the county of Asotin shall have one representative; the county of Chehalis shall have two representatives; the county of Clarke shall have three representatives; the county of Clallam shall have one representative; the county of Columbia shall have two representatives; the county of Cowlitz shall have one representative; the county of Douglas shall have one representative; the county of Franklin shall have one representative; the county of Garfield shall have one representative; the county of Island shall have one representative; the county of Jefferson shall have two representatives; the county of King shall have eight representatives; the county of Klickitat shall have two representatives; the county of Kittitas shall have two representatives; the county of Kitsap shall have one representative; the county of Lewis shall have two representatives; the county of Lincoln shall have two representatives; the county of Mason shall have one representative; the county of Okanogan shall have one representative; the county of Pacific shall have one representative; the county of Pierce shall have six representatives; the county of San Juan shall have one representative; the county of Skamania shall have one representative; the county of Snohomish shall have two representatives; the county of Skagit shall have two representatives; the county of Spokane shall have six representatives; the county of Stevens shall have one representative; the county of Thurston shall have two representatives; the county of Walla Walla shall have three representatives; the county of Wahkiakum shall have one representative; the county of Whatcom shall have two representatives; the county of Whitman shall have five representatives; the county of Yakima shall have one representative.

Article XXIII
Amendments

Section 1. How made. Any amendment or amendments to this Constitution may be proposed in either branch of the legislature; and if the same shall be agreed to by two-thirds of the members elected to each of the two houses, such proposed amendment or amendments shall be entered on their journals, with the ayes and noes thereon, and be submitted to the qualified electors of the state for their approval, at the next general election; and if the people approve and ratify such amendment or amendments, by a majority of the electors voting thereon, the same shall become part of this Constitution, and proclamation thereof shall be made by the governor: *Provided,* That if more than one amendment be submitted, they shall be submitted in such a manner that the people may vote for or against such amendments separately. The legislature shall also cause notice of the amendments that are to be submitted to the people to be published at least four times during the four weeks next preceding the election in every legal newspaper in the state: *Provided,* That failure of any newspaper to publish this notice shall not be interpreted as affecting the outcome of the election. [Amendment 37, 1961 Senate Joint Resolution No. 25, p 2753. Approved November, 1962.]

Section 2. Constitutional conventions. Whenever two-thirds of the members elected to each branch of the legislature shall deem it necessary to call a convention to revise or amend this Constitution, they shall recommend to the electors to vote at the next general election, for or against a convention, and if a majority of all the electors voting at said election shall have voted for a convention, the legislature shall at the next session, provide by law for calling the same; and such convention shall consist of a number of members, not less than that of the most numerous branch of the legislature.

Section 3. Submission to the people. Any Constitution adopted by such convention shall have no validity until it has been submitted to and adopted by the people.

Article XXIV
Boundaries

Section 1. State boundaries. The boundaries of the state
of Washington shall be as follows: Beginning at a point
in the Pacific ocean one marine league due west of and
opposite the middle of the mouth of the north ship channel
of the Columbia river thence running easterly to and up
the middle channel of said river and where it is divided
by islands up the middle of the widest channel thereof to
where the forty-sixth parallel of north latitude crosses
said river near the mouth of the Walla Walla river; thence
east on said forty-sixth parallel of latitude to the middle
of the main channel of Shoshone or Snake river, thence
follow down the middle of the main channel of Snake river
to a point opposite the mouth of the Kooskooskia or Clear
Water river, thence due north to the forty-ninth parallel of
north latitude, thence west along said forty-ninth parallel
of north latitude to the middle of the channel which
separates Vancouver's island from the continent, that
is to say to a point in longitude 123 degrees, 19 minutes
and 15 seconds west, thence following the boundary
line between the United States and British possessions
through the channel which separates Vancouver's island
from the continent to the termination of the boundary
line between the United States and British possessions at
a point in the Pacific ocean equidistant between Bonnilla
point on Vancouver's island and Tatoosh island light
house, thence running in a southerly course and parallel

with the coast line, keeping one marine league off shore to place of beginning; until such boundaries are modified by appropriate interstate compacts duly approved by the Congress of the United States. [Amendment 33, 1957 Senate Joint Resolution No. 10, p 1292. Approved November 4, 1958.]

Article XXV
Jurisdiction

Section 1. Authority of the United States. The consent of the State of Washington is hereby given to the exercise, by the congress of the United States, of exclusive legislation in all cases whatsoever over such tracts or parcels of land as are now held or reserved by the government of the United States for the purpose of erecting or maintaining thereon forts, magazines, arsenals, dockyards, lighthouses and other needful buildings, in accordance with the provisions of the seventeenth paragraph of the eighth section of the first article of the Constitution of the United States, so long as the same shall be so held and reserved by the United States. *Provided:* That a sufficient description by metes and bounds, and an accurate plat or map of each such tract or parcel of land be filed in the proper office of record in the county in which the same is situated, together with copies of the orders, deeds, patents or other evidences in writing of the title of the United States: *and provided,* That all civil process issued from the courts of this state and such criminal process as may issue under the authority of this state against any person charged with crime in cases arising outside of such reservations, may be served and executed thereon in the same mode and manner, and by the same officers, as if the consent herein given had not been made.

Article XXVI
Compact with the United States

The following ordinance shall be irrevocable without the consent of the United States and the people of this state:

First. That perfect toleration of religious sentiment shall be secured and that no inhabitant of this state shall ever be molested in person or property on account of his or her mode of religious worship.

Second. That the people inhabiting this state do agree and declare that they forever disclaim all right and title to the unappropriated public lands lying with the boundaries of this state, and to all lands lying within said limits owned or held by any Indian or Indian tribes; and that until the title thereto shall have been extinguished by the United States, the same shall be and remain subject to the disposition of the United States, and said Indian lands shall remain under the absolute jurisdiction and control of the congress of the United States and that the lands belonging to citizens of the United States residing without the limits of this state shall never be taxed at a higher rate than the lands belonging to residents thereof; and that no taxes shall be imposed by the state on lands or property therein, belonging to or which may be hereafter purchased by the United States or reserved for use: *Provided,* That nothing in this ordinance shall preclude the state from taxing as other lands are taxed any lands owned or held by any Indian who has severed his tribal relations, and has obtained from the United States or from any person a title thereto by patent or other grant, save and except such lands as have been or may be granted to any Indian or Indians under any act of congress containing a provision exempting the lands thus granted from taxation, which exemption shall continue so long and to such an extent as such act of congress may prescribe.

Third. The debts and liabilities of the Territory of Washington and payment of the same are hereby assumed by this state.

Fourth. Provision shall be made for the establishment and maintenance of systems of public schools free from sectarian control which shall be open to all the children of said state.

Article XXVII
Schedule

In order that no inconvenience may arise by reason of a change from a Territorial to a State government, it is hereby declared and ordained as follows:

Section 1. Existing rights, actions, and contracts saved. No existing rights, actions, suits, proceedings, contracts or claims shall be affected by a change in the form of government, but all shall continue as if no such change had taken place; and all process which may have been issued under the authority of the Territory of Washington previous to its admission into the Union shall be as valid as if issued in the name of the state.

Section 2. Laws in force continued. All laws now in force in the Territory of Washington, which are not repugnant to this Constitution, shall remain in force until they expire by their own limitation, or are altered or repealed by the legislature: *Provided,* That this section shall not be so construed as to validate any act of the legislature of Washington Territory granting shore or tide lands to any person, company or any municipal or private corporation.

Section 3. Debts, fines, etc., to inure to the state. All debts, fines, penalties and forfeitures, which have accrued, or may hereafter accrue, to the Territory of Washington, shall inure to the State of Washington.

Section 4. Recognizances. All recognizances heretofore taken, or which may be taken before the change from a territorial to a state government shall remain valid, and shall pass to, and may be prosecuted in the name of the state; and all bonds executed to the Territory of Washington or to any county or municipal corporation, or to any officer or court in his or its official capacity, shall pass to the state authorities and their successors in office, for the uses therein expressed, and may be sued for and recovered accordingly, and all the estate, real, personal and mixed, and all judgments decrees, bonds, specialties, choses in action, and claims or debts, of whatever description, belonging to the Territory of Washington, shall inure to and vest in the State of Washington, and may be sued for and recovered in the same manner, and to the same extent, by the State of Washington, as the same could have been by the Territory of Washington.

Section 5. Criminal prosecutions and penal actions. All criminal prosecutions and penal actions which may have arisen, or which may arise, before the change from a territorial to a state government, and which shall then be pending, shall be prosecuted to judgment, and execution in the name of the state. All offenses committed against the laws of the Territory of Washington, before the change from a territorial to a state government, and which shall not be prosecuted before such change, may be prosecuted in the name and by the authority of the State of Washington, with like effect as though such change had not taken place; and all penalties incurred shall remain the same as if this Constitution had not been adopted. All actions at law and suits in equity which may be pending in any of the courts of the Territory of Washington, at the time of the change from a territorial to a state government, shall be continued, and transferred to the court of the state having jurisdiction of the subject matter thereof.

Section 6. Retention of territorial officers. All officers now holding their office under the authority of the United States, or of the Territory of Washington, shall continue to hold and exercise their respective offices until they shall be superseded by the authority of the state.

Section 7. Constitutional officers, when elected. All officers provided for in this Constitution including a county clerk for each county when no other time is fixed for their election, shall be elected at the election to be held for the adoption of this Constitution on the first Tuesday of October, 1889.

Section 8. Change of courts – Transfer of causes. Whenever the judge of the superior court of any county, elected or appointed under the provisions of this Constitution shall have qualified the several causes then pending in the district court of the territory except such causes as would have been within the exclusive jurisdiction of the United States district court had such court existed at the time of the commencement of such causes, within such county, and the records, papers and proceedings of said district court, and the seal and other property pertaining thereto, shall pass into the jurisdiction and possession of the superior court for such county. And where the same judge is elected for two or more counties, it shall be the duty of the clerk of the district court having custody of such papers and records to transmit to the clerk of such county, or counties, other than that in which such records are kept the original papers in all cases pending in such district court and belonging to the jurisdiction of such county or counties together with transcript of so much of the records of said district court as relate to the same; and until the district courts of the Territory shall be superseded in manner aforesaid, the said district courts and the judges thereof, shall continue with the same jurisdiction and powers, to be exercised in the same judicial districts respectively, as heretofore constituted under the laws of the Territory. Whenever a quorum of the judges of the supreme court of the state shall have been elected and qualified, the causes then pending in the supreme court of the Territory, except such causes as would have been within the exclusive jurisdiction of the United States, circuit court had such court existed at the time of the commencement of such causes, and the papers, records and proceedings of said court and the seal and other property pertaining thereto, shall pass into the jurisdiction and possession of the supreme court of the state, and until so superseded, the supreme court of the Territory and the judges thereof, shall continue with like powers and jurisdiction as if this Constitution had not been adopted.

Section 9. Seals of courts and municipalities. Until otherwise provided by law, the seal now in use in the supreme court of the Territory shall be the seal of the supreme court of the state. The seals of the superior courts of the several counties of the state shall be, until otherwise provided by law, the vignette of General George Washington with the words: "Seal of the Superior Court of --------- county" surrounding the vignette. The seal of municipalities, and of all county officers of the Territory, shall be the seals of such municipalities, and county officers respectively under the state, until otherwise provided by law.

Section 10. Probate court, transfer of. When the state is admitted into the Union, and the superior courts in the respective counties organized, the books, records, papers and proceedings of the probate court in each county, and all causes and matters of administration pending therein, shall, upon the expiration of the term of office of the probate judges, on the second Monday in January, 1891, pass into the jurisdiction and possession of the superior court of the same county created by this Constitution, and the said court shall proceed to final judgment or decree, order or other determination in the several matters and causes, as the territorial probate court might have done, if this Constitution had not been adopted. And until the expiration of the term of office of the probate judges, such probate judges shall perform the duties now imposed upon them by the laws of the Territory. The superior courts shall have appellate and revisory jurisdiction over the decisions of the probate courts, as now provided by law, until such latter courts expire by limitation.

Section 11. Duties of first legislature. The legislature, at its first session, shall provide for the election of all officers whose election is not provided for elsewhere in this Constitution, and fix the time for the commencement and duration of their term.

Section 12. Election contests for superior judges, how decided. In case of a contest of election between candidates, at the first general election under this Constitution, for judges of the superior courts, the evidence shall be taken in the manner prescribed by the Territorial laws, and the testimony so taken shall be certified to the secretary of state; and said officer, together with the governor and treasurer of state, shall review the evidence and determine who is entitled to the certificate of election.

Section 13. Representation in congress. [Repealed by Amendment 74, 1983 Substitute Senate Joint Resolution No. 103. Approved November 8, 1983.]

Section 14. Duration of term of certain officers. All district, county and precinct officers, who may be in office at the time of the adoption of this Constitution, and the county clerk of each county elected at the first election, shall hold their respective offices until the second Monday of January, A. D., 1891, and until such time as their successors may be elected and qualified, in accordance with the provisions of this Constitution; and the official bonds of all such officers shall continue in full force and effect as though this Constitution had not been adopted. And such officers shall continue to receive the compensation now provided, until the same be changed by law.

Section 15. Election on adoption of constitution, how to be conducted. The election held at the time of the adoption of this Constitution shall be held and conducted in all respects according to the laws of the Territory, and the votes cast at said election for all officers (where no other provisions are made in this Constitution), and for the adoption of this Constitution and the several separate articles and the location of the state capital, shall be canvassed and returned in the several counties in the manner provided by Territorial law, and shall be returned to the secretary of the Territory in the manner provided by the Enabling Act.

Section 16. When constitution to take effect. The provisions of this Constitution shall be in force from the day on which the president of the United States shall issue his proclamation declaring the State of Washington admitted into the Union, and the terms of all officers elected at the first election under the provisions of this Constitution shall commence on the Monday next succeeding the issue of said proclamation, unless otherwise provided herein.

Section 17. Separate articles. The following separate articles shall be submitted to the people for adoption or rejection at the election for the adoption of this Constitution:

Separate Article, No. 1

"All persons male and female of the age of twenty-one years or over, possessing the other qualifications, provided by this Constitution, shall be entitled to vote at all elections."

Separate Article, No. 2

"It shall not be lawful for any individual, company or corporation, within the limits of this state, to manufacture, or cause to be manufactured, or to sell, or offer for sale, or in any manner dispose of any alcoholic, malt or spirituous liquors, except for medicinal, sacramental or scientific purposes."

If a majority of the ballots cast at said election on said separate articles be in favor of the adoption of either of said separate articles, then such separate article so receiving a majority shall become a part of this

Constitution and shall govern and control any provision of
the Constitution in conflict therewith.

Section 18. Ballot. The form of ballot to be used in
voting for or against this Constitution, or for or against
the separate articles, or for the permanent location of the
seat of government, shall be:

For the Constitution.../
Against the Constitution ....

For Woman Suffrage Article.../
Against Woman Suffrage Article....................................

For Prohibition Article ..../
Against Prohibition Article...

For the Permanent Location of the Seat of Government
(Name of place voted for)..

Section 19. Appropriation. The legislature is hereby authorized to appropriate from the state treasury sufficient
money to pay any of the expenses of this convention not
provided for by the Enabling Act of Congress.

Article XXVIII
Compensation of State Officers

Section 1. Salaries for legislature, elected state officials, and judges – Independent commission – Referendum. Salaries for members of the legislature, elected officials of the executive branch of state government, and judges of the state's supreme court, court of appeals, superior courts, and district courts shall be fixed by an independent commission created and directed by law to that purpose. No state official, public employee, or person required by law to register with a state agency as a lobbyist, or immediate family member of the official, employee, or lobbyist, may be a member of that commission.

As used in this section the phrase "immediate family" has the meaning that is defined by law.

Any change of salary shall be filed with the secretary of state and shall become law ninety days thereafter without action of the legislature or governor, but shall be subject to referendum petition by the people, filed within the ninety-day period. Referendum measures under this section shall be submitted to the people at the next following general election, and shall be otherwise governed by the provisions of this Constitution generally applicable to referendum measures. The salaries fixed pursuant to this section shall supersede any other provision for the salaries of members of the legislature, elected officials of the executive branch of state government, and judges of the state's supreme court, court of appeals, superior courts, and district courts. The salaries for such officials in effect on January 12, 1987, shall remain in effect until changed pursuant to this section.

After the initial adoption of a law by the legislature creating the independent commission, no amendment to such act which alters the composition of the commission shall be valid unless the amendment is enacted by a favorable vote of two-thirds of the members elected to each house of the legislature and is subject to referendum petition.

The provisions of section 14 of Article IV, sections 14, 16, 17, 19, 20, 21, and 22 of Article III, and section 23 of Article II, insofar as they are inconsistent herewith, are hereby superseded. The provisions of section 1 of Article II relating to referendum procedures, insofar as they are inconsistent herewith, are hereby superseded with regard to the salaries governed by this section. [Amendment 78, 1986 Substitute House Joint Resolution No. 49, p 1529. Approved November 4, 1986.]

Article XXIX
Investments of Public Pension and Retirement Funds

Section 1. May be invested as authorized by law. Notwithstanding the provisions of sections 5, and 7 of Article VIII and section 9 of Article XII or any other section or article of the Constitution of the state of Washington, the moneys of any public pension or retirement fund, industrial insurance trust fund, or fund held in trust for the benefit of persons with developmental disabilities may be invested as authorized by law. [Amendment 93, 2000 Senate Joint Resolution No. 8214, p 1919. Approved November 7, 2000.]

Article XXX
Compensation of Public Officers

Section 1. Authorizing compensation increase during term. The compensation of all elective and appointive state, county, and municipal officers who do not fix their own compensation, including judges of courts of record and the justice courts may be increased during their terms of office to the end that such officers and judges shall each severally receive compensation for their services in accordance with the law in effect at the time the services are being rendered.

The provisions of section 25 of Article II (Amendment 35), section 25 of Article III (Amendment 31), section 13 of Article IV, section 8 of Article XI, and section 1 of Article XXVIII (Amendment 20) insofar as they are inconsistent herewith are hereby repealed. [Amendment 54, 1967 House Joint Resolution No. 13; see 1969 p 2976. Approved November 5, 1968.]

Article XXXI
Sex Equality - Rights and Responsibilities

Section 1. Equality not denied because of sex. Equality of rights and responsibility under the law shall not be denied or abridged on account of sex.

Section 2. Enforcement power of legislature. The legislature shall have the power to enforce, by appropriate legislation, the provisions of this article. [Amendment 61, 1972 House Joint Resolution No. 61, p 526. Approved November, 1972.]

Article XXXII
Special Revenue Financing

Section 1. Special revenue financing. The legislature may enact laws authorizing the state, counties, cities, towns, port districts, or public corporations established thereby to issue nonrecourse revenue bonds or other nonrecourse revenue obligations and to apply the proceeds thereof in the manner and for the purposes heretofore or hereafter authorized by law, subject to the following limitations:

(a) Nonrecourse revenue bonds and other nonrecourse revenue obligations issued pursuant to this section shall be payable only from money or other property received as a result of projects financed by the nonrecourse revenue bonds or other nonrecourse revenue obligations and from money and other property received from private sources.

(b) Nonrecourse revenue bonds and other nonrecourse revenue obligations issued pursuant to this section shall not be payable from or secured by any tax funds or governmental revenue or by all or part of the faith and credit of the state or any unit of local government.

(c) Nonrecourse revenue bonds or other nonrecourse revenue obligations issued pursuant to this section may be issued only if the issuer certifies that it reasonably believes that the interest paid on the bonds or obligations will be exempt from income taxation by the federal government.

(d) Nonrecourse revenue bonds or other nonrecourse revenue obligations may only be used to finance industrial development projects as defined in legislation.

(e) The state, counties, cities, towns, port districts, or public corporations established thereby, shall never exercise their respective attributes of sovereignty, including but not limited to, the power to tax, the power of eminent domain, and the police power on behalf of any industrial development project authorized pursuant to this section.

After the initial adoption of a law by the legislature authorizing the issuance of nonrecourse revenue bonds or other nonrecourse revenue obligations, no amendment to such act which expands the definition of industrial development project shall be valid unless the amendment is enacted by a favorable vote of three-fifths of the members elected to each house of the legislature and is subject to referendum petition.

Sections 5 and 7 of Article VIII and section 9 of Article XII shall not be construed as a limitation upon the authority granted by this section. The proceeds of revenue bonds and other revenue obligations issued pursuant to this section for the purpose of financing privately owned property or loans to private persons or corporations shall be subject to audit by the state but shall not otherwise be deemed to be public money or public property for purposes of this Constitution. This section is supplemental to and shall not be construed as a repeal of or limitation on any other authority lawfully exercisable under the Constitution and laws of this state, including, among others, any existing authority to issue revenue bonds. [Amendment 73, 1981 Substitute House Joint Resolution No. 7, p 1794. Approved November 3, 1981.]

The Constitution of the United States of America

We the People of the United States, in Order to form a more perfect Union, establish Justice, insure domestic Tranquillity, provide for the common defense, promote the general Welfare, and secure the Blessings of Liberty to ourselves and our Posterity, do ordain and establish this Constitution for the United States of America.

Article I

Section 1

All legislative Powers herein granted shall be vested in a Congress of the United States, which shall consist of a Senate and House of Representatives.

Section 2

The House of Representatives shall be composed of Members chosen every second Year by the People of the several States, and the Electors in each State shall have the Qualifications requisite for Electors of the most numerous Branch of the State Legislature.

No Person shall be a Representative who shall not have attained to the Age of twenty five Years, and been seven Years a Citizen of the United States, and who shall not, when elected, be an Inhabitant of that State in which he shall be chosen.

Representatives and direct Taxes shall be apportioned among the several States which may be included within this Union, according to their respective Numbers, which shall be determined by adding to the whole Number of free Persons, including those bound to Service for a Term of Years, and excluding Indians not taxed, three fifths of all other Persons. The actual Enumeration shall be made within three Years after the first Meeting of the Congress of the United States, and within every subsequent Term of ten Years, in such Manner as they shall by Law direct. The Number of Representatives shall not exceed one for every thirty Thousand, but each State shall have at Least one Representative; and until such enumeration shall be made, the State of New Hampshire shall be entitled to chuse three, Massachusetts eight, Rhode-Island and Providence Plantations one, Connecticut five, New-York six, New Jersey four, Pennsylvania eight, Delaware one, Maryland six, Virginia ten, North Carolina five, South Carolina five, and Georgia three.

When vacancies happen in the Representation from any State, the Executive Authority thereof shall issue Writs of Election to fill such Vacancies.

The House of Representatives shall chuse their Speaker and other Officers; and shall have the sole Power of Impeachment.

Section 3

The Senate of the United States shall be composed of two Senators from each State, chosen by the Legislature thereof, for six Years; and each Senator shall have one Vote.

Immediately after they shall be assembled in Consequence of the first Election, they shall be divided as equally as may be into three Classes. The Seats of the Senators of the first Class shall be vacated at the Expiration of the second Year, of the second Class at the Expiration of the fourth Year, and of the third Class at the Expiration of the sixth Year, so that one third may be chosen every second Year; and if Vacancies happen by Resignation, or otherwise, during the Recess of the Legislature of any State, the Executive thereof may make temporary Appointments until the next Meeting of the Legislature, which shall then fill such Vacancies.

No Person shall be a Senator who shall not have attained to the Age of thirty Years, and been nine Years a Citizen of the United States, and who shall not, when elected, be an Inhabitant of that State for which he shall be chosen.

The Vice President of the United States shall be President of the Senate, but shall have no Vote, unless they be equally divided.

The Senate shall chuse their other Officers, and also a President pro tempore, in the Absence of the Vice President, or when he shall exercise the Office of President of the United States.

The Senate shall have the sole Power to try all Impeachments. When sitting for that Purpose, they shall be on Oath or Affirmation. When the President of the United States is tried, the Chief Justice shall preside: And no Person shall be convicted without the Concurrence of two thirds of the Members present.

Judgment in Cases of Impeachment shall not extend further than to removal from Office, and disqualification to hold and enjoy any Office of honor, Trust or Profit under the United States: but the Party convicted shall nevertheless be liable and subject to Indictment, Trial, Judgment and Punishment, according to Law.

Section 4

The Times, Places and Manner of holding Elections for Senators and Representatives, shall be prescribed in each State by the Legislature thereof; but the Congress may at any time by Law make or alter such Regulations, except as to the Places of chusing Senators.

The Congress shall assemble at least once in every Year, and such Meeting shall be on the first Monday in December, unless they shall by Law appoint a different Day.

Section 5

Each House shall be the Judge of the Elections, Returns and Qualifications of its own Members, and a Majority of each shall constitute a Quorum to do Business; but a smaller Number may adjourn from day to day, and may be authorized to compel the Attendance of absent Members, in such Manner, and under such Penalties as each House may provide.

Each House may determine the Rules of its Proceedings, punish its Members for disorderly Behaviour, and, with the Concurrence of two thirds, expel a Member.

Each House shall keep a Journal of its Proceedings, and from time to time publish the same, excepting such Parts as may in their Judgment require Secrecy; and the Yeas and Nays of the Members of either House on any question shall, at the Desire of one fifth of those Present, be entered on the Journal.

Neither House, during the Session of Congress, shall, without the Consent of the other, adjourn for more than three days, nor to any other Place than that in which the two Houses shall be sitting.

Section 6

The Senators and Representatives shall receive a Compensation for their Services, to be ascertained by Law, and paid out of the Treasury of the United States. They shall in all Cases, except Treason, Felony and Breach of the Peace, be privileged from Arrest during their Attendance at the Session of their respective Houses, and in going to and returning from the same; and for any Speech or Debate in either House, they shall not be questioned in any other Place.

No Senator or Representative shall, during the Time for which he was elected, be appointed to any civil Office under the Authority of the United States, which shall have been created, or the Emoluments whereof shall have been encreased during such time; and no Person holding any Office under the United States, shall be a Member of either House during his Continuance in Office.

Section 7

All Bills for raising Revenue shall originate in the House of Representatives; but the Senate may propose or concur with Amendments as on other Bills.

Every Bill which shall have passed the House of Representatives and the Senate, shall, before it become a Law, be presented to the President of the United States;

If he approve he shall sign it, but if not he shall return it, with his Objections to that House in which it shall have originated, who shall enter the Objections at large on their Journal, and proceed to reconsider it. If after such Reconsideration two thirds of that House shall agree to pass the Bill, it shall be sent, together with the Objections, to the other House, by which it shall likewise be reconsidered, and if approved by two thirds of that House, it shall become a Law. But in all such Cases the Votes of both Houses shall be determined by Yeas and Nays, and the Names of the Persons voting for and against the Bill shall be entered on the Journal of each House respectively, If any Bill shall not be returned by the President within ten Days (Sundays excepted) after it shall have been presented to him, the Same shall be a Law, in like Manner as if he had signed it, unless the Congress by their Adjournament prevent its Return, in which Case it shall not be a Law.

Every Order, Resolution, or Vote to which the Concurrence of the Senate and House of Representatives may be necessary (except on a question of Adjournment) shall be presented to the President of the United States; and before the Same shall take Effect, shall be approved by him, or being disapproved by him, shall be repassed by two thirds of the Senate and House of Representatives, according to the Rules and Limitations prescribed in the Case of a Bill.

Section 8

The Congress shall have Power To lay and collect Taxes, Duties, Imposts and Excises, to pay the Debts and provide for the common Defence and general Welfare of the United States; but all Duties, Imposts and Excises shall be uniform throughout the United States;

> To borrow Money on the credit of the United States;

> To regulate Commerce with foreign Nations, and among the several States, and with the Indian Tribes;

> To establish an uniform Rule of Naturalization, and uniform Laws on the subject of Bankruptcies throughout the United States;

> To coin Money, regulate the Value thereof, and of foreign Coin, and fix the Standard of Weights and Measures;

> To provide for the Punishment of counterfeiting the Securities and current Coin of the United States;

> To establish Post Offices and post Roads;

> To promote the Progress of Science and useful Arts, by securing for limited Times to Authors and Inventors the exclusive Right to their respective Writings and Discoveries;

To constitute Tribunals inferior to the supreme Court;

To define and punish Piracies and Felonies committed on the high Seas, and Offences against the Law of Nations;

To declare War, grant Letters of Marque and Reprisal, and make Rules concerning Captures on Land and Water;

To raise and support Armies, but no Appropriation of Money to that Use shall be for a longer Term than two Years;

To provide and maintain a Navy;

To make Rules for the Government and Regulation of the land and naval Forces;

To provide for calling forth the Militia to execute the Laws of the Union, suppress Insurrections and repel Invasions;

To provide for organizing, arming, and disciplining, the Militia, and for governing such Part of them as may be employed in the Service of the United States, reserving to the States respectively, the Appointment of the Officers, and the Authority of training the Militia according to the discipline prescribed by Congress;

To exercise exclusive Legislation in all Cases
  whatsoever, over such District (not exceeding ten Miles square) as may, by Cession
  of particular States, and the Acceptance of
  Congress, become the Seat of the Government of the United States, and to exercise
  like Authority over all Places purchased by
  the Consent of the Legislature of the State in
  which the Same shall be, for the Erection of
  Forts, Magazines, Arsenals, dock-Yards and
  other needful Buildings;-And

To make all Laws which shall be necessary
  and proper for carrying into Execution the
  foregoing Powers, and all other Powers vested
  by this Constitution in the Government of
  the United States, or in any Department or
  Officer thereof.

Section 9

The Migration or Importation of such Persons as any of
the States now existing shall think proper to admit, shall
not be prohibited by the Congress prior to the Year one
thousand eight hundred and eight, but a Tax or duty may
be imposed on such Importation, not exceeding ten dollars for each Person.

The Privilege of the Writ of Habeas Corpus shall not be suspended, unless when in Cases of Rebellion or Invasion the public Safety may require it.

No Bill of Attainder or ex post facto Law shall be passed.

No Capitation, or other direct, Tax shall be laid, unless in Proportion to the Census or Enumeration herein before directed to be taken.

No Tax or Duty shall be laid on Articles exported from any State.

No Preference shall be given by any Regulation of Commerce or Revenue to the Ports of one State over those of another: nor shall Vessels bound to, or from, one State, be obliged to enter, clear, or pay Duties in another.

No Money shall be drawn from the Treasury, but in Consequence of Appropriations made by Law; and a regular Statement and Account of the Receipts and Expenditures of all public Money shall be published from time to time.

No Title of Nobility shall be granted by the United States: And no Person holding any Office of Profit or Trust under them, shall, without the Consent of the Congress, accept of any present, Emolument, Office, or Title, of any kind whatever, from any King, Prince, or foreign State.

Section 10

No State shall enter into any Treaty, Alliance, or Confederation; grant Letters of Marque and Reprisal; coin Money; emit Bills of Credit; make any Thing but gold and silver Coin a Tender in Payment of Debts; pass any Bill of Attainder, ex post facto Law, or Law impairing the Obligation of Contracts, or grant any Title of Nobility.

No State shall, without the Consent of the Congress, lay any Imposts or Duties on Imports or Exports, except what may be absolutely necessary for executing it's inspection Laws: and the net Produce of all Duties and Imposts, laid by any State on Imports or Exports, shall be for the Use of the Treasury of the United States; and all such Laws shall be subject to the Revision and Controul of the Congress.

No State shall, without the Consent of Congress, lay any Duty of Tonnage, keep Troops, or Ships of War in time of Peace, enter into any Agreement or Compact with another State, or with a foreign Power, or engage in War, unless actually invaded, or in such imminent Danger as will not admit of delay.

Article II

Section 1

The executive Power shall be vested in a President of the United States of America. He shall hold his Office during the Term of four Years, and, together with the Vice President, chosen for the same Term, be elected, as follows:

Each State shall appoint, in such Manner as the Legislature thereof may direct, a Number of Electors, equal to the whole Number of Senators and Representatives to which the State may be entitled in the Congress: but no Senator or Representative, or Person holding an Office of Trust or Profit under the United States, shall be appointed an Elector.

The Electors shall meet in their respective States, and vote by Ballot for two Persons, of whom one at least shall not be an Inhabitant of the same State with themselves. And they shall make a List of all the Persons voted for, and of the Number of Votes for each; which List they shall sign and certify, and transmit sealed to the Seat of the Government of the United States, directed to the President of the Senate. The President of the Senate shall, in the Presence of the Senate and House of Representatives, open all the Certificates, and the Votes shall then be counted. The Person having the greatest Number of Votes shall be the President, if such Number be a Majority of the whole Number of Electors appointed; and if there be more than one who have such Majority, and have an equal

Number of Votes, then the House of Representatives shall immediately chuse by Ballot one of them for President; and if no Person have a Majority, then from the five highest on the List the said House shall in like Manner chuse the President. But in chusing the President, the Votes shall be taken by States, the Representation from each State having one Vote; A quorum for this Purpose shall consist of a Member or Members from two thirds of the States, and a Majority of all the States shall be necessary to a Choice. In every Case, after the Choice of the President, the Person having the greatest Number of Votes of the Electors shall be the Vice President. But if there should remain two or more who have equal Votes, the Senate shall chuse from them by Ballot the Vice President.

The Congress may determine the Time of chusing the Electors, and the Day on which they shall give their Votes; which Day shall be the same throughout the United States.

No Person except a natural born Citizen, or a Citizen of the United States, at the time of the Adoption of this Constitution, shall be eligible to the Office of President; neither shall any person be eligible to that Office who shall not have attained to the Age of thirty five Years, and been fourteen Years a Resident within the United States.

In Case of the Removal of the President from Office, or of his Death, Resignation, or Inability to discharge the Powers and Duties of the said Office, the Same shall devolve on the Vice President, and the Congress may by

Law provide for the Case of Removal, Death, Resignation or Inability, both of the President and Vice President, declaring what Officer shall then act as President, and such Officer shall act accordingly, until the Disability be removed, or a President shall be elected.

The President shall, at stated Times, receive for his Services, a Compensation, which shall neither be increased nor diminished during the Period for which he shall have been elected, and he shall not receive within that Period any other Emolument from the United States, or any of them. Before he enter on the Execution of his Office, he shall take the following Oath or Affirmation:—"I do solemnly swear (or affirm) that I will faithfully execute the Office of President of the United States, and will to the best of my Ability, preserve, protect and defend the Constitution of the United States."

Section 2

The President shall be Commander in Chief of the Army and Navy of the United States, and of the Militia of the several States, when called into the actual Service of the United States; he may require the Opinion, in writing, of the principal Officer in each of the executive Departments, upon any Subject relating to the Duties of their respective Offices, and he shall have Power to grant Reprieves and Pardons for Offenses against the United States, except in Cases of Impeachment.

He shall have Power, by and with the Advice and Consent of the Senate, to make Treaties, provided two thirds of the Senators present concur; and he shall nominate, and by and with the Advice and Consent of the Senate, shall appoint Ambassadors, other public Ministers and Consuls, Judges of the supreme Court, and all other Officers of the United States, whose Appointments are not herein otherwise provided for, and which shall be established by Law: but the Congress may by Law vest the Appointment of such inferior Officers, as they think proper, in the President alone, in the Courts of Law, or in the Heads of Departments.

The President shall have Power to fill up all Vacancies that may happen during the Recess of the Senate, by granting Commissions which shall expire at the End of their next Session.

Section 3

He shall from time to time give to the Congress Information of the State of the Union, and recommend to their Consideration such Measures as he shall judge necessary and expedient; he may, on extraordinary Occasions, convene both Houses, or either of them, and in Case of Disagreement between them, with Respect to the Time of Adjournment, he may adjourn them to such Time as he shall think proper; he shall receive Ambassadors and other public Ministers; he shall take Care that the Laws be faithfully executed, and shall Commission all the Officers of the United States.

Section 4

The President, Vice President and all civil Officers of the United States, shall be removed from Office on Impeachment for, and Conviction of, Treason, Bribery, or other high Crimes and Misdemeanors.

Article III

Section 1

The judicial Power of the United States, shall be vested in one supreme Court, and in such inferior Courts as the Congress may from time to time ordain and establish. The Judges, both of the supreme and inferior Courts, shall hold their Offices during good Behaviour, and shall at stated Times, receive for their Services, a Compensation, which shall not be diminished during their Continuance in Office.

Section 2

The judicial Power shall extend to all Cases, in Law and Equity, arising under this Constitution, the Laws of the United States, and Treaties made, or which shall be made, under their Authority;—to all Cases affecting Ambassadors, other public Ministers and Consuls;—to all Cases of admiralty and maritime Jurisdiction;—to Controversies to which the United States shall be a Party;—to Controversies between two or more States;—between a State and Citizens of another State;—between Citizens of different States,—between Citizens of the same State claiming Lands under Grants of different States, and between a State, or the Citizens thereof;—and foreign States, Citizens or Subjects.

In all Cases affecting Ambassadors, other public Ministers and Consuls, and those in which a State shall be Party, the supreme Court shall have original Jurisdiction. In all the other Cases before mentioned, the supreme Court shall have appellate Jurisdiction, both as to Law and Fact, with such Exceptions, and under such Regulations as the Congress shall make.

The Trial of all Crimes, except in Cases of Impeachment; shall be by Jury; and such Trial shall be held in the State where the said Crimes shall have been committed; but when not committed within any State, the Trial shall be at such Place or Places as the Congress may by Law have directed.

Section 3

Treason against the United States, shall consist only in levying War against them, or in adhering to their Enemies, giving them Aid and Comfort. No Person shall be convicted of Treason unless on the Testimony of two Witnesses to the same overt Act, or on Confession in open Court.

The Congress shall have Power to declare the Punishment of Treason, but no Attainder of Treason shall work Corruption of Blood, or Forfeiture except during the Life of the Person attainted.

Article IV

Section 1

Full Faith and Credit shall be given in each State to the public Acts, Records, and judicial Proceedings of every other State. And the Congress may by general Laws prescribe the Manner in which such Acts, Records and Proceedings shall be proved, and the Effect thereof.

Section 2

The Citizens of each State shall be entitled to all Privileges and Immunities of Citizens in the several States.

A Person charged in any State with Treason, Felony, or other Crime, who shall flee from Justice, and be found in another State, shall on Demand of the executive Authority of the State from which he fled, be delivered up, to be removed to the State having Jurisdiction of the Crime.

No Person held to Service or Labour in one State, under the Laws thereof, escaping into another, shall, in Consequence of any Law or Regulation therein, be discharged from such Service or Labour, but shall be delivered up on Claim of the Party to whom such Service or Labour may be due.

Section 3

New States may be admitted by the Congress into this Union; but no new State shall be formed or erected within the Jurisdiction of any other State; nor any State be formed by the Junction of two or more States, or Parts of States, without the Consent of the Legislatures of the States concerned as well as of the Congress.

The Congress shall have Power to dispose of and make all needful Rules and Regulations respecting the Territory or other Property belonging to the United States; and nothing in this Constitution shall be so construed as to Prejudice any Claims of the United States, or of any particular State.

Section 4

The United States shall guarantee to every State in this Union a Republican Form of Government, and shall protect each of them against Invasion; and on Application of the Legislature, or of the Executive (when the Legislature cannot be convened) against domestic Violence.

Article V

The Congress, whenever two thirds of both Houses shall deem it necessary, shall propose Amendments to this Constitution, or, on the Application of the Legislatures of two thirds of the several States, shall call a Convention for proposing Amendments, which in either Case, shall be valid to all Intents and Purposes, as Part of this Constitution, when ratified by the Legislatures of three-fourths of the several States, or by Conventions in three fourths thereof, as the one or the other Mode of Ratification may be proposed by the Congress; Provided that no Amendment which may be made prior to the Year One thousand eight hundred and eight shall in any Manner affect the first and fourth Clauses in the Ninth Section of the first Article; and that no State, without its Consent, shall be deprived of its equal Suffrage in the Senate.

Article VI

All Debts contracted and Engagements entered into, before the Adoption of this Constitution, shall be as valid against the United States under this Constitution, as under the Confederation.

This Constitution, and the Laws of the United States which shall be made in Pursuance thereof; and all Treaties made, or which shall be made, under the Authority of the United States, shall be the supreme Law of the Land; and the Judges in every State shall be bound thereby, any Thing in the Constitution or Laws of any State to the Contrary notwithstanding.

The Senators and Representatives before mentioned, and the Members of the several State Legislatures, and all executive and judicial Officers, both of the United States and of the several States, shall be bound by Oath or Affirmation, to support this Constitution; but no religious Test shall ever be required as a Qualification to any Office or public Trust under the United States.

Article VII

The Ratification of the Conventions of nine States, shall be sufficient for the Establishment of this Constitution between the States so ratifying the Same.

done in Convention by the Unanimous Consent of the States present the Seventeenth Day of September in the Year of our Lord one thousand seven hundred and Eighty seven and of the Independence of the United States of America the Twelfth In Witness whereof We have hereunto subscribed our Names,

Attest William Jackson   Go. Washington--Presidt:
Secretary   and deputy from Virginia

New Hampshire

John Langdon   Nicholas Gilman

Massachusetts

Nathaniel Gorham   Rufus King

Connecticut

Wm. Saml. Johnson   Roger Sherman

New York

Alexander Hamilton

New Jersey

Wil: Livingston   Wm. Paterson
David Brearley   Jona: Dayton

Pennsylvania

B Franklin   Thos. FitzSimons
Thomas Mifflin   Jared Ingersoll
Robt Morris   James Wilson
Geo. Clymer   Gouv Morris

Delaware

Geo: Read   Richard Bassett
Gunning Bedford jun   Jaco: Broom
John Dickinson

Maryland

James McHenry   Danl Carroll
Dan of St. Thos. Jenifer

Virginia

John Blair   James Madison Jr.

North Carolina

Wm. Blount   Hu Williamson
Richd. Dobbs Spaight

South Carolina

J. Rutledge   Charles Pinckney
Pierce Butler   Charles Cotesworth Pinckney

Georgia

William Few   Abr Baldwin

In Convention Monday
September 17th, 1787.

Present

The States of New Hampshire, Massachusetts, Connecticut, Mr. Hamilton from New York, New Jersey, Pennsylvania, Delaware, Maryland, Virginia, North Carolina, South Carolina and Georgia.

Resolved,

That the preceeding Constitution be laid before the United States in Congress assembled, and that it is the Opinion of this Convention, that it should afterwards be submitted to a Convention of Delegates, chosen in each State by the People thereof, under the Recommendation of its Legislature, for their Assent and Ratification; and that each Convention assenting to, and ratifying the Same, should give Notice thereof to the United States in Congress assembled. Resolved, That it is the Opinion of this Convention, that as soon as the Conventions of nine States shall have ratified this Constitution, the United States in Congress assembled should fix a Day on which Electors should be appointed by the States which shall have ratified the same, and a Day on which the Electors should assemble to vote for the President, and the Time and Place for commencing Proceedings under this Constitution. That after such Publication the Electors should be appointed, and the Senators and Representatives elected: That the Electors should meet on the Day fixed for the Election of the President, and should transmit their Votes certified, signed, sealed and directed, as the Constitution requires, to the Secretary of the United States in Congress assembled, that the Senators and Representatives should convene at the Time and Place assigned; that the Senators should appoint a President of the Senate, for the sole Purpose of receiving, opening and counting the Votes for President; and, that after he shall be chosen, the Congress, together with the President, should, without Delay, proceed to execute this Constitution.

> By the Unanimous Order of the Convention
> Go. Washington-Presidt:
> W. Jackson Secretary.

Preamble to the Bill of Rights

Congress of the United States begun and held at the City of New-York, on Wednesday the fourth of March, one thousand seven hundred and eighty nine

THE Conventions of a number of the States, having at the time of their adopting the Constitution, expressed a desire, in order to prevent misconstruction or abuse of its powers, that further declaratory and restrictive clauses should be added: And as extending the ground of public confidence in the Government, will best ensure the beneficent ends of its institution.

RESOLVED by the Senate and House of Representatives of the United States of America, in Congress assembled, two thirds of both Houses concurring, that the following Articles be proposed to the Legislatures of the several States, as amendments to the Constitution of the United States, all, or any of which Articles, when ratified by three fourths of the said Legislatures, to be valid to all intents and purposes, as part of the said Constitution; viz. ARTICLES in addition to, and Amendment of the Constitution of the United States of America, proposed by Congress, and ratified by the Legislatures of the several States, pursuant to the fifth Article of the original Constitution.

Amendment I

Congress shall make no law respecting an establishment of religion, or prohibiting the free exercise thereof; or abridging the freedom of speech, or of the press, or the right of the people peaceably to assemble, and to petition the Government for a redress of grievances.

Amendment II

A well regulated Militia, being necessary to the security of a free State, the right of the people to keep and bear Arms, shall not be infringed.

Amendment III

No Soldier shall, in time of peace be quartered in any house, without the consent of the Owner, nor in time of war, but in a manner to be prescribed by law.

Amendment IV

The right of the people to be secure in their persons, houses, papers, and effects, against unreasonable searches and seizures, shall not be violated, and no Warrants shall issue, but upon probable cause, supported by Oath or affirmation, and particularly describing the place to be searched, and the persons or things to be seized.

Amendment V

No person shall be held to answer for a capital, or otherwise infamous crime, unless on a presentment or indictment of a Grand Jury, except in cases arising in the land or naval forces, or in the Militia, when in actual service in time of War or public danger; nor shall any person be subject for the same offence to be twice put in jeopardy of life or limb; nor shall be compelled in any criminal case to be a witness against himself, nor be deprived of life, liberty, or property, without due process of law; nor shall private property be taken for public use, without just compensation.

Amendment VI

In all criminal prosecutions, the accused shall enjoy the right to a speedy and public trial, by an impartial jury of the State and district wherein the crime shall have been committed, which district shall have been previously ascertained by law, and to be informed of the nature and cause of the accusation; to be confronted with the witnesses against him; to have compulsory process for obtaining witnesses in his favor, and to have the Assistance of Counsel for his defence.

Amendment VII

In Suits at common law, where the value in controversy shall exceed twenty dollars, the right of trial by jury shall be preserved, and no fact tried by a jury shall be otherwise reexamined in any Court of the United States, than according to the rules of the common law.

Amendment VIII

Excessive bail shall not be required, nor excessive fines imposed, nor cruel and unusual punishments inflicted.

Amendment IX

The enumeration in the Constitution, of certain rights, shall not be construed to deny or disparage others retained by the people.

Amendment X

The powers not delegated to the United States by the Constitution, nor prohibited by it to the States, are reserved to the States respectively, or to the people.

✢ ✢ ✢

Amendments 11-27

Amendment XI

Passed by Congress March 4, 1794. Ratified February 7, 1795.

The Judicial power of the United States shall not be construed to extend to any suit in law or equity, commenced or prosecuted against one of the United States by Citizens of another State, or by Citizens or Subjects of any Foreign State.

Amendment XII

Passed by Congress December 9, 1803. Ratified June 15, 1804.

The Electors shall meet in their respective states, and vote by ballot for President and Vice-President, one of whom, at least, shall not be an inhabitant of the same state with themselves; they shall name in their ballots the person voted for as President, and in distinct ballots the person voted for as Vice-President, and they shall make distinct lists of all persons voted for as President, and of all persons voted for as Vice-President, and of the number of votes for each, which lists they shall sign and certify, and transmit sealed to the seat of the government of the United States, directed to the President of the Senate;—the President of the Senate shall, in the presence of the Senate and House of Representatives, open all the certificates and the votes shall then be counted;—The person having the greatest number of votes for President, shall be the President, if such number be a majority of the whole number of Electors appointed; and if no person have such majority, then from the persons having the highest numbers not exceeding three on the list of those voted for as President, the House of Representatives shall choose immediately, by ballot, the President. But in choosing the President, the votes shall be taken by states, the representation from each state having one vote; a quorum for this purpose shall consist of a member or members from two-thirds of the states, and a majority of all the states shall be necessary to a choice. And if the House of Representatives shall not choose a President whenever the right of choice shall devolve upon them, before the fourth day of March next following, then the Vice-President shall act as President, as in case of the death or other constitutional disability of the President. The person having the greatest number of votes as Vice-President, shall be the Vice-President, if such number be a majority of the whole number of Electors appointed, and if no person have a majority, then from the two highest numbers on the list, the Senate shall choose the Vice-President; a quorum for the purpose shall consist of two-thirds of the whole number of Senators, and a majority of the whole number shall be necessary to a choice. But no person constitutionally ineligible to the office of President shall be eligible to that of Vice-President of the United States.

Amendment XIII

Passed by Congress January 31, 1865. Ratified December 6, 1865.

Section 1.

Neither slavery nor involuntary servitude, except as a punishment for crime whereof the party shall have been duly convicted, shall exist within the United States, or any place subject to their jurisdiction.

Section 2.

Congress shall have power to enforce this article by appropriate legislation.

Amendment XIV

Passed by Congress June 13, 1866. Ratified July 9, 1868.

Section 1.

All persons born or naturalized in the United States and subject to the jurisdiction thereof, are citizens of the United States and of the State wherein they reside. No State shall make or enforce any law which shall abridge the privileges or immunities of citizens of the United States; nor shall any State deprive any person of life, liberty, or property, without due process of law; nor deny to any person within its jurisdiction the equal protection of the laws.

Section 2.

Representatives shall be apportioned among the several States according to their respective numbers, counting the whole number of persons in each State, excluding Indians not taxed. But when the right to vote at any election for the choice of electors for President and Vice President of the United States, Representatives in Congress, the Executive and Judicial officers of a State, or the members of the Legislature thereof, is denied to any of the male inhabitants of such State, being twenty-one years of age, and citizens of the United States, or in any way abridged, except for participation in rebellion, or other crime, the basis of representation therein shall be reduced in the proportion which the number of such male citizens shall bear to the whole number of male citizens twenty-one years of age in such State.

Section 3.

No person shall be a Senator or Representative in Congress, or elector of President and Vice President, or hold any office, civil or military, under the United States, or under any State, who, having previously taken an oath, as a member of Congress, or as an officer of the United States, or as a member of any State legislature, or as an executive or judicial officer of any State, to support the Constitution of the United States, shall have engaged in insurrection or rebellion against the same, or given aid or comfort to the enemies thereof. But Congress may by a vote of two-thirds of each House, remove such disability.

Section 4.

The validity of the public debt of the United States, authorized by law, including debts incurred for payment of pensions and bounties for services in suppressing insurrection or rebellion, shall not be questioned. But neither the United States nor any State shall assume or pay any debt or obligation incurred in aid of insurrection or rebellion against the United States, or any claim for the loss or emancipation of any slave; but all such debts, obligations and claims shall be held illegal and void.

Section 5.

The Congress shall have the power to enforce, by appropriate legislation, the provisions of this article.

Amendment XV

Passed by Congress February 26, 1869. Ratified February 3, 1870.

Section 1.

The right of citizens of the United States to vote shall not be denied or abridged by the United States or by any State on account of race, color, or previous condition of servitude.

Section 2.

The Congress shall have the power to enforce this article by appropriate legislation.

Amendment XVI

Passed by Congress July 2, 1909. Ratified February 3, 1913.

The Congress shall have power to lay and collect taxes on incomes, from whatever source derived, without apportionment among the several States, and without regard to any census or enumeration.

Amendment XVII

Passed by Congress May 13, 1912. Ratified April 8, 1913.

The Senate of the United States shall be composed of two Senators from each State, elected by the people thereof, for six years; and each Senator shall have one vote. The electors in each State shall have the qualifications requisite for electors of the most numerous branch of the State legislatures.

When vacancies happen in the representation of any State in the Senate, the executive authority of such State shall issue writs of election to fill such vacancies: Provided, That the legislature of any State may empower the executive thereof to make temporary appointments until the people fill the vacancies by election as the legislature may direct.

This amendment shall not be so construed as to affect the election or term of any Senator chosen before it becomes valid as part of the Constitution.

Amendment XVIII

Passed by Congress December 18, 1917. Ratified January 16, 1919. Repealed by the 21st Amendment, December 5, 1933.

Section 1.

After one year from the ratification of this article the manufacture, sale, or transportation of intoxicating liquors within, the importation thereof into, or the exportation thereof from the United States and all territory subject to the jurisdiction thereof for beverage purposes is hereby prohibited.

Section 2.

The Congress and the several States shall have concurrent power to enforce this article by appropriate legislation.

Section 3.

This article shall be inoperative unless it shall have been ratified as an amendment to the Constitution by the legislatures of the several States, as provided in the Constitution, within seven years from the date of the submission hereof to the States by the Congress.

Amendment XIX

Passed by Congress June 4, 1919. Ratified August 18, 1920.

The right of citizens of the United States to vote shall not be denied or abridged by the United States or by any State on account of sex.

Congress shall have power to enforce this article by appropriate legislation.

Amendment XX

Passed by Congress March 2, 1932. Ratified January 23, 1933.

Section 1.

The terms of the President and the Vice President shall end at noon on the 20th day of January, and the terms of Senators and Representatives at noon on the 3d day of January, of the years in which such terms would have ended if this article had not been ratified; and the terms of their successors shall then begin.

Section 2.

The Congress shall assemble at least once in every year, and such meeting shall begin at noon on the 3d day of January, unless they shall by law appoint a different day.

Section 3.

If, at the time fixed for the beginning of the term of the President, the President elect shall have died, the Vice President elect shall become President. If a President shall not have been chosen before the time fixed for the beginning of his term, or if the President elect shall have failed to qualify, then the Vice President elect shall act as President until a President shall have qualified; and the Congress may by law provide for the case wherein neither a President elect nor a Vice President shall have qualified, declaring who shall then act as President, or the manner in which one who is to act shall be selected, and such person shall act accordingly until a President or Vice President shall have qualified.

Section 4.

The Congress may by law provide for the case of the death of any of the persons from whom the House of Representatives may choose a President whenever the right of choice shall have devolved upon them, and for the case of the death of any of the persons from whom the Senate may choose a Vice President whenever the right of choice shall have devolved upon them.

Section 5.

Sections 1 and 2 shall take effect on the 15th day of October following the ratification of this article.

Section 6.

This article shall be inoperative unless it shall have been ratified as an amendment to the Constitution by the legislatures of three-fourths of the several States within seven years from the date of its submission.

Amendment XXI

Passed by Congress February 20, 1933. Ratified December 5, 1933.

Section 1.

The eighteenth article of amendment to the Constitution of the United States is hereby repealed.

Section 2.

The transportation or importation into any State, Territory, or possession of the United States for delivery or use therein of intoxicating liquors, in violation of the laws thereof, is hereby prohibited.

Section 3.

This article shall be inoperative unless it shall have been ratified as an amendment to the Constitution by conventions in the several States, as provided in the Constitution, within seven years from the date of the submission hereof to the States by the Congress.

Amendment XXII

Passed by Congress March 21, 1947. Ratified February 27, 1951.

Section 1.

No person shall be elected to the office of the President more than twice, and no person who has held the office of President, or acted as President, for more than two years of a term to which some other person was elected President shall be elected to the office of President more than once.

But this Article shall not apply to any person holding the office of President when this Article was proposed by Congress, and shall not prevent any person who may be holding the office of President, or acting as President, during the term within which this Article becomes operative from holding the office of President or acting as President during the remainder of such term.

Section 2.

This article shall be inoperative unless it shall have been ratified as an amendment to the Constitution by the legislatures of three-fourths of the several States within seven years from the date of its submission to the States by the Congress.

Amendment XXIII

Passed by Congress June 16, 1960. Ratified March 29, 1961.

Section 1.

The District constituting the seat of Government of the United States shall appoint in such manner as Congress may direct:

A number of electors of President and Vice President equal to the whole number of Senators and Representatives in Congress to which the District would be entitled if it were a State, but in no event more than the least populous State; they shall be in addition to those appointed by the States, but they shall be considered, for the purposes of the election of President and Vice President, to be electors appointed by a State; and they shall meet in the District and perform such duties as provided by the twelfth article of amendment.

Section 2.

The Congress shall have power to enforce this article by appropriate legislation.

Amendment XXIV

Passed by Congress August 27, 1962. Ratified January 23, 1964.

Section 1.

The right of citizens of the United States to vote in any primary or other election for President or Vice President, for electors for President or Vice President, or for Senator or Representative in Congress, shall not be denied or abridged by the United States or any State by reason of failure to pay poll tax or other tax.

Section 2.

The Congress shall have power to enforce this article by appropriate legislation.

Amendment XXV

Passed by Congress July 6, 1965. Ratified February 10, 1967.

Section 1.

In case of the removal of the President from office or of his death or resignation, the Vice President shall become President.

Section 2.

Whenever there is a vacancy in the office of the Vice President, the President shall nominate a Vice President who shall take office upon confirmation by a majority vote of both Houses of Congress.

Section 3.

Whenever the President transmits to the President pro tempore of the Senate and the Speaker of the House of Representatives his written declaration that he is unable to discharge the powers and duties of his office, and until he transmits to them a written declaration to the contrary, such powers and duties shall be discharged by the Vice President as Acting President.

Section 4.

Whenever the Vice President and a majority of either the principal officers of the executive departments or of such other body as Congress may by law provide, transmit to the President pro tempore of the Senate and the Speaker of the House of Representatives their written declaration that the President is unable to discharge the powers and duties of his office, the Vice President shall immediately assume the powers and duties of the office as Acting President.

Thereafter, when the President transmits to the President pro tempore of the Senate and the Speaker of the House of Representatives his written declaration that no inability exists, he shall resume the powers and duties of his office unless the Vice President and a majority of either the principal officers of the executive department or of such other body as Congress may by law provide, transmit within four days to the President pro tempore of the Senate and the Speaker of the House of Representatives their written declaration that the President is unable to discharge the powers and duties of his office. Thereupon Congress shall decide the issue, assembling within forty-eight hours for that purpose if not in session. If the Congress, within twenty-one days after receipt of the latter written declaration, or, if Congress is not in session, within twenty-one days after Congress is required to assemble, determines by two-thirds vote of both Houses that the President is unable to discharge the powers and duties of his office, the Vice President shall continue to discharge the same as Acting President; otherwise, the President shall resume the powers and duties of his office.

Amendment XXVI

Passed by Congress March 23, 1971. Ratified July 1, 1971.

Section 1.

The right of citizens of the United States, who are eighteen years of age or older, to vote shall not be denied or abridged by the United States or by any State on account of age.

Section 2.

The Congress shall have power to enforce this article by appropriate legislation.

Amendment XXVII

Ratified May 7, 1992.

No law, varying the compensation for the services of the
Senators and Representatives, shall take effect, until an
election of representatives shall have intervened.

About Us

Advancing individual liberty, free enterprise, and limited accountable government—that is the mission of the Freedom Foundation. Our work is focused in many areas, including budget and taxes, business and labor, education, election integrity, property rights, constitutional law, and first principles. The Freedom Foundation seeks to expose corruption, stand up against waste, and tell citizens the truth about government policies.

We aim to engage, educate, and empower citizens to be leaders for freedom in our state and in our nation. Freedom Foundation accomplishments include:

- Restoration of the voices of property owners whose property rights were restricted through local regulations;

- Promotion of the expansion of public online learning options in Washington State based on research that proves online learning positively impacts the way students learn;

- Preservation efforts to save Federalism and the Electoral College through educating people on the myths of the National Popular Vote;

- Promotion of open government through media and litigation; and

- Dedication to connecting, equipping, and mobilizing the people of Washington State to help keep freedom alive by engaging them directly with the government.

We envision a day when opportunity, responsible self-governance, and free markets flourish in Washington State because its citizens understand and cherish the principles from which freedom is derived. You may learn more about the Freedom Foundation and our projects at www.myfreedomfoundation.org

The Freedom Foundation is a nonprofit think tank that does not accept any funds from government sources. We rely solely on the voluntary support of citizens.